RECIPE for MURDER

ESTÉRELLE PAYANY
ILLUSTRATIONS BY JEAN-FRANÇOIS MARTIN

FRIGHTFULLY GOOD FOOD
INSPIRED BY FICTION

RECIPE for MURDER

Flammarion

CONTENTS

THE DELICACY OF CRIME

I must admit that it's a strange idea: peering at all of literature's "bad guys," villains, and shady characters from the rim
of a saucepan. "Oh, I would kill for a taste of that!" Literally.

Where does one draw the line between criminal—in the
strictly legal sense of the term—and hero? Romeo kills
Tybalt in a moment of fury; Julien Sorel shoots Madame de
Rênal*; Meursault** kills the first person he comes across.
Yet, I'm sure you've long forgotten that they all could have
answered for their wrongful deeds before a court of law.

In literature as in the movies, bad guys are always the most
fascinating characters to analyze and decipher. Whether they
are perpetrators of parricide, theft, murder, or wide-scale
organized crime, criminals offer us a complex reflection of
their nature: at times, it appears monstrous and inexcusable;
at other times, all too human and understandable.

* Julien Sorel, the protagonist in Stendhal's *The Red and the Black* (1830), shoots—but does not kill—his
former lover, Madame de Rênal, during Mass.
** In Albert *Camus*' *The Outsider*, published in 1942, Frenchman Meursault kills an Arab man in Algiers for
apparently no reason.

All criminals possess that same witch-like ambiguity. Isn't Medea above all a derided woman who has lost everything? Does Lady Macbeth do anything other than utter what has been lurking deep inside her husband's unconscious all along?

In the end, this rather dark cast has made room for a few laughs and surprises. How could one not leave a special spot at the table for that infamous consumer of human beings (I almost wrote, human beans), Hannibal Lecter? Or overlook Roald Dahl's delectable Mary, who kills her husband by hitting him over the head with a frozen leg of lamb? Did you know that there's a cake named after Othello? Or that Dracula knew how to prepare chicken? Can you picture Lady Macbeth slipping on an apron before concocting a batch of her poisonous possets? Maybe you and the Queen of Hearts share a passion for treacle tart?

The time has come to get to the heart of the matter. So put down your pens and get out your (kitchen) knives!

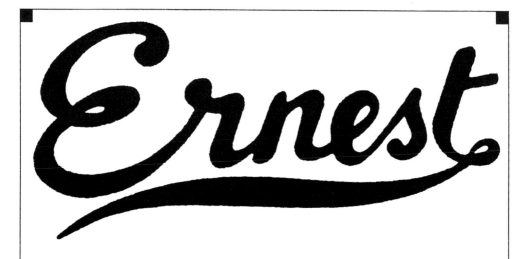

Ernest

Ernest, an evolved hominid, recounts the story of his tribe, from the first gatherers to the discovery of fire by his father, Edward, "the greatest ape-man of the Pleistocene,"* and an enthusiast for evolution and inventions. Weary of his father's limitless imagination, which he finds to be dangerous, Ernest ends up committing the archetypal symbolic act: killing his father and eating him, so that a piece of his genius lives on in those who follow.

* 214.

" To widen one's feeding habits from the purely vegetarian (and almost wholly frugivorous at that) towards omnivorousness is a painful and difficult process, demanding immense patience and persistence in discovering how to keep things down which not only disgust one, but disagree with one as well. Only unrelenting ambition, the desire to improve one's place in nature, and ruthless self-discipline will carry one through that transition. I am not denying that there are unexpected tidbits to be found, but life cannot be all snails and sweetbreads. Once you set out to be omnivorous you must learn to eat *everything*, and in times when you never know where the next meal is coming from you must also eat everything *up*. As children we were brought up most strictly on these rules; and a child who dared to say, 'But, Mummy, I don't like toad!' was a child asking to have its ears boxed. 'Eat it up; it's good for you,' was the refrain of my childhood.*"

Ernest – *Evolution Man: Or, How I Ate My Father*, **Roy Lewis** (1960)

A PLEISTOCENE MARROWBONE

Sharpen some flints, and blacken your wooden spears
in the fire to make them more menacing.
Go on a hunt with your father and brothers, while
the womenfolk tend the fire.
Run and track down anything that looks edible: bison, buffalo,
impalas, oryx, wildebeests, gazelles, hartebeests, zebras. If all
else fails, you can always go after rabbits, badgers, or squirrels.
Though they're a sure bet, they're not as tasty or filling.
Eat to your heart's content right on the scene of the kill: skin
and joint the beast; feast on the blood, intestines, and brain
(a choice piece of meat that any well-evolved ape-man would
save for his father). Quarter your game with your flints and
carry it triumphantly back to the cave.
Be sure to eat all the meat; thoroughly chew the raw flesh.
Split open the bones, and suck the marrow with gusto.
If you're having a gala, serve your bounty alongside
mammoth ribs, escalopes of chalicotherium, a haunch
of zebra, or even a boar's head.

* 16–17.

OPEN-FACE MARROWBONE SANDWICHES

Ingredients for 4 servings:

2 lb (1 kg) marrowbones (beef or veal)
3 tablespoons coarse salt
1 bay leaf
4 generous slices of country-style bread
2 cloves garlic, peeled

Ask your butcher to section the bones.

Rub the ends of each bone in coarse salt, so that the marrow stays inside.

Add the bay leaf to 12 cups (3 liters) water, and bring to a boil. **POACH** the bones over moderate heat for 1 hour.

Lightly toast the bread, and rub it with garlic.

Remove the marrow from the bones, and **SPREAD** it over the warm bread.

Serve immediately with a green salad and well-seasoned vinaigrette.

Giants with one or three eyes (depending on the legend you hear), Cyclops were builders before becoming shepherds.

The most famous of all is Polyphemus ("he who speaks much"), the son of Poseidon, who tends to his sheep in Sicily. A cannibal living in a remote cave, with an enormous rock as a door, Polyphemus delights in taking bites out of some of Ulysses' buddies. Using all of his cunning, Ulysses intoxicates the Cyclops with wine before boring his eye out with a burning-hot stake. Then Ulysses and his men manage to escape from the cave right under Polyphemus' nose by hanging onto the bellies of his sheep. Yet another reason for Poseidon to want to get even with Ulysses!

But the Cyclops didn't disappear with antiquity. He resurfaces in the Pyrenees under the name of Tartaro. Popular Basque tales share a striking similarity with Homer's story: the Cyclops always ends up fooled and blinded, while the valorous hero(s) use(s) animals to escape. A bit farther away, in Gascony and Béarn, the pastoral giant is named Bécut and tends to a flock of rams with golden horns.

These metamorphoses of Polyphemus bridge the gap between the myth of the Cyclops and that of the ogre who feasts upon raw flesh.

Now should you come upon a place where shepherds have been tending their flocks for centuries, you can be sure that a legend of the Cyclops looms nearby.

"As soon as he had put the stone back to its place against the door, he sat down, milked his ewes and his goats all quite rightly, and then let each have her own young one; when he had got through with all this work, he gripped up two more of my men, and made his supper off them. So I went up to him with an ivy-wood bowl of black wine in my hands:

'Look here, Cyclops,' said I, you have been eating a great deal of man's flesh, so take this and drink some wine, that you may see what kind of liquor we had on board my ship. I was bringing it to you as a drink-offering, in the hope that you would take compassion upon me and further me on my way home, whereas all you do is to go on ramping and raving most intolerably. You ought to be ashamed of yourself; how can you expect people to come see you any more if you treat them in this way?'

He then took the cup and drank. He was so delighted with the taste of the wine that he begged me for another bowl full. 'Be so kind,' he said, 'as to give me some more, and tell me your name at once. I want to make you a present that you will be glad to have. We have wine even in this country, for our soil grows grapes and the sun ripens them, but this drinks like nectar and ambrosia all in one.'

I then gave him some more; three times did I fill the bowl for him, and three times did he drain it without thought or heed; then, when I saw that the wine had got into his head, I said to him as plausibly as I could: 'Cyclops, you ask my name and I will tell it you; give me, therefore, the present you promised me; my name is Noman; this is what my father and mother and my friends have always called me.'

But the cruel wretch said, 'Then I will eat all Noman's comrades before Noman himself, and will keep Noman for the last. This is the present that I will make him.'*"

Cyclops – *The Odyssey*, **Homer (around 800 BCE)**

* English translation by Samuel Butler, Book 9.

CYCLOPS-STYLE SHOULDER OF LAMB

Ingredients for 4–6 servings:

1 shoulder baby lamb (about 3lb or 1.25 kg)
3 ½ tablespoons olive oil
6 cloves garlic
1 teaspoon Espelette pepper
2 onions
1 bay leaf, crumbled
½ cup (100 ml) Amaro Averna*
Salt and pepper

Begin marinating the lamb as soon as rosy-fingered Dawn appears.

CUT small incisions in the surface of the lamb.

Peel, degerm, and **MINCE** the garlic cloves. Mix the olive oil, garlic, Espelette pepper, and a pinch of salt and pepper in a crater (a bowl will do the job, too). Rub the shoulder of lamb with this mixture. Then cover the lamb, and refrigerate it for at least 6 hours, or even an entire day.

Ideally, you would then cook it on the **SPIT**, preferably over "burning cedar and sandal wood." Otherwise, an oven preheated to 350°F (180°C) will work just fine.

PEEL AND MINCE the onions before spreading them over the bottom of a lightly greased braising pan. Arrange the shoulder of lamb on the bed of onions, and sprinkle with Amaro and the **CRUMBLED** bay leaf.

Cook the lamb for 30 minutes. Turn the meat over, and baste the lamb generously with the pan juices. Cook for another 30 minutes.

As Homer said: "By and by, when the other meats were roasted and had been taken off the spits, the **CARVERS** gave every man his portion and they all made an exellent dinner.»

SERVE PIPING HOT!

* Amaro Averna is a traditional Sicilian liqueur made from nearly sixty different herbs and produced in Caltanissetta, located in the heart of Sicily. If you don't have any Amaro handy, you can substitute a myrtle liqueur, known as *mirto* in Sardinia and Corsica.

MEDEA

Filled with tumult and fury, the mythical persona of Medea has inspired a great number of literary works since ancient times and continues to unleash passion in her readers. An enchantress and the daughter of the king of Colchis (part of present-day Georgia), she embodies all the mystery and magic of the East.

When she falls in love with the handsome Jason, she uses her sorcery to help him conquer the Golden Fleece and then marries her hero. They go off to live happily ever after in Corinth ... until Jason starts coveting the king's throne and falls in love with—surprise, surprise—the king's daughter.

Finding herself forsaken by the very hero she so willingly sacrificed her own brother's life for, Medea is not about to give up now. She poisons Jason's new fiancée, as well as the king. And then, in order to leave Jason heirless and ensure that they die by no one else's hand, Medea resolves to kill her own children.

An alien in Greece, Medea left everything behind for love. She's a barbarian who reverts to her primitive state the day Jason's affections cool. Her destructive rage is all she has left to feel alive. She is no longer a wife, and rather than give the society that excludes her the satisfaction of making her an outlaw, she chooses to exclude herself by committing the most unforgivable of crimes.

Unnatural and monstrous mother, or driven and courageous foreigner: every era has its own version of the myth.

" Curses on thee! Now perceive what then I missed in the day I brought thee, fraught with doom, from thy home in a barbarian land to dwell in Hellas, traitress to thy sire and to the land that nurtured thee. On me the gods have hurled the curse that dogged thy steps, for thou didst slay thy brother at his hearth ere thou cam'st aboard our fair ship, Argo. Such was the outset of thy life of crime; then didst thou wed with me, and having borne me sons to glut thy passion's lust, thou now hast slain them. Not one amongst the wives of Hellas e'er had dared this deed; yet before them all I chose thee for my wife, wedding a foe to be my doom, no woman, but a lioness fiercer than Tyrrhene Scylla in nature.* "

Medea – *Medea*, Euripides (431 BCE)

* English translation by E.P. Coleridge.

KOLIVA

A mixture of wheat, sugar, seeds, and spices, koliva is prepared during funeral services and on certain holidays in Greece as homage to the dead. It's not something people eat for fun.

Laden with religious symbols, koliva can be traced back to Anthesteria, an Athenian festival, which celebrated Dionysus with a mixture of cereal grains and nuts, symbolizing life and death. Some have even claimed that these festivals were initiated by Theseus, the mythical king of Athens, who, incidentally, also had a bone to pick with Medea. He was, after all, the son of Aegeus, whom she married after Jason.

Due to its drab appearance, koliva is usually heavily decorated. A candle is sometimes placed in the middle and lit at the beginning of a ceremony. If the Orthodox don't approve of serving Koliva for breakfast, then eat it with respect—and with a kind thought for the victims of Medea's fury.

Ingredients for a large dish of koliva (6 servings):

1⅓ cups (200 g) soft wheat berries (found in health food stores)
1 cup (50 g) dried breadcrumbs
¼ cup (50 g) sugar
1 handful raisins
1 handful coarsely ground walnuts
1 handful ground almonds
Seeds from 1 pomegranate
2 tablespoons sesame seeds
1 teaspoon aniseed
1 teaspoon ground cinnamon
Salt
For decoration: confectioner's sugar, whole almonds, and walnuts

A day ahead: thoroughly **RINSE** the wheat berries
under cold water. Then cover the wheat with lightly salted
water in a pan and let **SIMMER** for 1 hour.

•

DRAIN thoroughly and dry in a clean dishcloth.

•

The next day: pour the wheat into a large bowl,
and stir in the breadcrumbs and sugar.
Then add all the other ingredients, mixing well.

•

Arrange the koliva evenly in a serving bowl,
and sprinkle with powdered sugar.

•

Top with walnuts, sugared almonds, or any other edible decorations

THAT SUIT YOUR FANCY!

BRUTUS

●

During antiquity alone, over eleven authors relayed the bloody end of Julius Caesar, who was assassinated in the middle of the Senate in 44 BCE when a group of senators, including Caesar's adopted son, Brutus, stabbed him twenty-three times.

Depending on which author you read, Brutus is either a champion of Roman democracy or a monstrous parricide.

But Caesar's own political ambiguity cannot be overlooked. When he was named dictator for life, many feared he had ambitions to become king. Brutus may have killed his foster father, but did this same act of violence save the Republic?

Dante* leaves Brutus in Lucifer's hands, in the darkest depths of Hell, alongside traitors like Judas and Cassius, Caesar's co-assassin. Others, such as Voltaire**, have found a place for him somewhere between love of country and love of family: a difficult choice to make.

A champion of the public interest or a deviant son, Brutus is a true hero according to Mark Antony in Shakespeare's *Julius Caesar*: "He, only in a general honest thought / And common good to all, made one of them."***

Nevertheless, Brutus has been sentenced to remain on the sidelines of literature: not a single title bears his name. Be it Rex Warner's *Imperial Caesar* (1960) or Shakespeare's *Julius Caesar* (in which the eponymous character dies in Act 3), the works that feature him seem to confine Brutus to the shadows of parricide.

* The Divine Comedy, Canto XXXIV, 1308–21.
** *The Death of Caesar*, 1736.
*** 5.5.2756–7.

"As he took his seat, the conspirators gathered about him as if to pay their respects, and straightway Tillius Cimber, who had assumed the lead, came nearer as though to ask something; and when Caesar with a gesture put him off to another time, Cimber caught his toga by both shoulders; then as Caesar cried, 'Why, this is violence!' one of the Cascas stabbed him from one side just below the throat. Caesar caught Casca's arm and ran it through with his stylus, but as he tried to leap to his feet, he was stopped by another wound. When he saw that he was beset on every side by drawn daggers, he muffled his head in his robe, and at the same time drew down its lap to his feet with his left hand, in order to fall more decently, with the lower part of his body also covered. And in this wise he was stabbed with three and twenty wounds, uttering not a word, but merely a groan at the first stroke, though some have written that when Marcus Brutus rushed at him, he said in Greek, 'You too, my child?' All the conspirators made off, and he lay there lifeless for some time, and finally three common slaves put him on a litter and carried him home, with one arm hanging down. And of so many wounds none turned out to be mortal, in the opinion of the physician Antistius, except the second one in the breast.*"

Brutus – *The Lives of the Twelve Caesars*, **Suetonius (probably written during Hadrian's reign: 117–138 CE)**

* English translation by J.C. Rolfe.

THE REAL CAESAR SALAD

No, Julius Caesar didn't eat Caesar salad. Food wasn't even his thing. According to Cato the Younger, he lived practically like an ascetic (at least in this one respect): Caesar was the only one to plot the republic's ruin on an empty stomach.

Chef Caesar Cardini created this typically American dish in 1924 at Hotel Caesar's in Tijuana, Mexico, where Cardini's restaurant business was free from the restrictions of prohibition. On the Fourth of July in 1924, the hotel's restaurant was so packed that Cardini decided to improvise with what he had on hand: lettuce, olive oil, Parmesan cheese, and eggs. And since the kitchen was over-crowded, he decided to wing it right in front of his customers—causing an immediate hit. Clark Gable, Jean Harlow, and W. C. Fields were soon racing down to Tijuana for a bite of the famous "closet" salad that took neither vinegar nor anchovies, contrary to many of today's versions.

Ingredients for 4 servings:

4 cloves garlic
⅔ cup (150 ml) extra-virgin olive oil
2 slices (80 g) day-old bread
2 heads romaine lettuce
½ cup (80 g) high-quality Parmesan cheese, freshly grated or in shavings

For the dressing:
2 one-minute eggs
Juice from 2 lemons
10 drops Worcestershire sauce
½ teaspoon salt
½ teaspoon pepper

Prepare the garlic-infused oil at least three days ahead. **PEEL** and degerm the garlic, and **CUT** into thick slices. Add the garlic to the olive oil in an airtight container. Then close, and leave to infuse for three days at room temperature. On the day you make the salad, preheat the oven to 300°F (150°C).

•

Prepare the croutons by removing the crust from the bread. Then **DICE** the bread, and with a pastry brush, cover each crouton with the garlic-infused oil. **COOK** the croutons in the oven, turning often to make sure they don't burn.

Select and wash the lettuce leaves, then carefully spin them dry. Tip them into a large salad bowl.

Add the salt and pepper and remaining garlic-infused oil. Then **CRACK** the eggs right onto the lettuce, and add the lemon juice and Worcestershire sauce.

•

Gently toss the salad until the dressing become creamy and coats the lettuce evenly.

•

Add the Parmesan and croutons, and toss the salad once more before serving.

23

AGRIPPINA

With time, Agrippina, the sister of Caligula (Emperor of Rome, 37–41 CE), wife of Claudius (Emperor of Rome, 42–54 CE), and mother of Nero (Emperor of Rome, 54–68 CE), has evolved into somewhat of a mythical character.

Supposedly, the delicious Agrippina assassinated (among other atrocities—but should one really believe everything said by Tacitus' vicious tongue?) her husband, the Emperor Claudius—who happened to be her uncle as well—in order to free the throne for Nero, the rightful descendant.

According to Tacitus, the dish that finally did for Claudius was made from *delectabili boleto*—which should not be translated by ordinary "boletus mushrooms." The *boleto* that was so treasured by emperors had an inviting orange cap and was named, in the emperors' honor, *Amanita caesarea*. It is also said that emperors used these mushrooms as an aphrodisiac: As long as you're eating lying down, why not mix in a few other pleasures? For once, Pliny the Elder, Martial, Juvenal, and Suetonius are all in agreement: it was indeed a mushroom orgy that gave Agrippina the perfect opportunity to do away with her husband. Alas, Caesar's mushrooms have a close—and deadly—cousin, *Amanita phalloides*, which, despite their name, are not an aphrodisiac. And due to their similar tastes, the two mushrooms, one poisonous and the other delicious, could easily have been blended together.

Nero knew all too well how indebted he was to Agrippina. When Caesar's mushrooms were being served at a banquet, Nero heard a guest cite the Greek proverb, "Mushrooms are the food of the gods," only to reply: "That's right. It was from eating a mushroom that my father became a god."[*] Had you forgotten that all Roman emperors were deified when they died?

[*] Patrick Faas, *Around the Roman Table*, 236; English translation by Sean Whiteside.

"All the circumstances were subsequently so well known, that writers of the time have declared that the poison was infused into some mushrooms, a favourite delicacy, and its effect not at the instant perceived, from the emperor's lethargic, or intoxicated condition. His bowels too were relieved, and this seemed to have saved him. Agrippina was thoroughly dismayed. Fearing the worst, and defying the immediate obloquy of the deed, she availed herself of the complicity of Xenophon, the physician, which she had already secured. Under pretence of helping the emperor's efforts to vomit, this man, it is supposed, introduced into his throat a feather smeared with some rapid poison; for he knew that the greatest crimes are perilous in their inception, but well rewarded after their consummation."*

Agrippina (15–59 CE) – *Annals*, **Tacitus (109 CE)**

* English translation by Alfred John Church and William Jackson Brodribb.

AGRIPPINA'S MUSHROOMS

Although this isn't an authentic Roman recipe (especially in the way it's cooked), it does rely on flavors and ingredients from Ancient Rome. Nuoc mam, a Vietnamese fish sauce, is the closest thing we have to *garum*, the fermented fish sauce that the Romans used instead of salt. And honey works magic in reproducing the sweet-and-sour taste the Romans loved. Fresh herbs were used in everything, but they were pretty different from the ones we use today. Instead of parsley and basil, lovage, rue, wild fennel, and different varieties of mint were added to food. Peppermint or pennyroyal could be used in this recipe—but if you're set on finding some, you'd better be prepared to get a little dirty!

Ingredients for 4 servings:

1 lb (600 g) Caesar's mushrooms (button or boletus mushrooms can be used instead)
1 tablespoon olive oil
1 tablespoon nuoc mam
1 tablespoon honey
1 sprig peppermint

Wipe the mushrooms clean with a damp dishcloth or pastry brush.

•

SLICE them thinly.

•

HEAT the olive oil over a medium flame, and lightly sauté the mushrooms, stirring frequently, until they give off their water.

•

Add the nuoc mam and honey.
Stir, and cook for 5 minutes.

•

In the meantime, wash, dry, and **CHOP** the peppermint.

•

Remove the sauté pan from the heat, and add the peppermint.
Stir, and serve as a side dish with roast poultry or meat.

•

LIE BACK AND ENJOY!

Lady MACBETH

It's difficult to have to choose from the catalog of bloodthirsty Shakespearean characters! But in this particular festival of atrocities, written in the grandest of poetic styles, Lady Macbeth, inspired by the real-life Queen Gruoch of Scotland, who reigned during the eleventh century, deserves our undivided attention.

Often seen as a cutthroat, power-hungry manipulator who incites her husband to kill Duncan before going insane and committing suicide out of guilt, Lady Macbeth is both a dominant and dominated character. She and her husband make a complex couple, with Lady Macbeth showing the courage that her husband lacks (and even the balls, I'd say, based on passages like this: "unsex me here, / And fill me from the crown to the toe top-full / Of direst cruelty!"*). All she does is utter his deepest desires—a kind of superego incarnate who helps him realize his dreams. Once she is queen, though, Lady Macbeth's resolve fades fast: all she wanted was for her husband's power to make him happy, but instead, it ends up crushing him. A woman in love is above all a woman of extremes: a witch (she does poison people after all) and murderess in one.

In the end, the gore of Macbeth is nothing compared to that of Titus Andronicus, in which an insane emperor literally makes mincemeat out of his enemies, before cooking their heads into a delicate pie and serving it to their mother.

They definitely knew what eating was all about during the Elizabethan era!

* 1.5.391–3.

LADY MACBETH. My royal lord, / You do not give the cheer: the feast is sold / That is not often vouch'd, while 'tis a-making, / 'Tis given with welcome: to feed were best at home; / From thence the sauce to meat is ceremony; / Meeting were bare without it.

MACBETH. Sweet remembrancer! / Now good digestion wait on appetite, / And health on both!

LENNOX. May't please your highness sit.

(*The Ghost of BANQUO enters, and sits in MACBETH's place.*)

MACBETH. Here had we now our country's honor roof'd, / Were the graced person of our Banquo present; / Who may I rather challenge for unkindness / Than pity for mischance!

ROSS. His absence, sir, / Lays blame upon his promise. Please't your highness / To grace us with your royal company.

MACBETH. The table's full.

LENNOX. Here is a place reserved, sir.

MACBETH. Where?

LENNOX. Here, my good lord. What is't that moves your highness?

MACBETH. Which of you have done this?

LORDS. What, my good lord?

MACBETH. Thou canst not say I did it: never shake / Thy gory locks at me.

ROSS. Gentlemen, rise: his highness is not well.

LADY MACBETH. Sit, worthy friends: my lord is often thus, / And hath been from his youth: pray you, keep seat; / The fit is momentary; upon a thought / He will again be well: if much you note him, / You shall offend him and extend his passion: / Feed, and regard him not. Are you a man?

MACBETH. Ay, and a bold one, that dare look on that / Which might appal the devil.

LADY MACBETH. O proper stuff! / This is the very painting of your fear: / This is the air-drawn dagger which, you said, / Led you to Duncan. O, these flaws and starts, / Impostors to true fear, would well become / A woman's story at a winter's fire, / Authorized by her grandam. Shame itself! / Why do you make such faces? When all's done, / You look but on a stool.

MACBETH. Prithee, see there! behold! look! lo! / how say you? / Why, what care I? If thou canst nod, speak too. / If charnel-houses and our graves must send / Those that we bury back, our monuments / Shall be the maws of kites.

(*The Ghost of BANQUO vanishes.*)

LADY MACBETH. What, quite unmann'd in folly?*

Lady Macbeth – *Macbeth*, **Shakespeare (written between 1603 and 1607, the story takes place sometime around 1040)**

*3.4.1311–63.

LADY MACBETH'S POSSETS

Lady Macbeth's culinary talents are fully divulged in her single-handed efforts to poison Duncan's guards: "I have drugg'd / their possets, / That death and nature do contend about them, / Whether they live or die."*

A posset is a creamy drink of hot milk sweetened with honey and curdled with wine or ale. Its comforting nature made it a favorite pick-me-up, much like cordial or a glass of warm milk today, for someone feeling under the weather or in want of a good night's sleep.

Since the sixteenth century, possets have gradually become enriched with eggs and thickened over the stove—often with a hearty dollop of cream—making them more like pudding than an invigorating milk punch.

★

Ingredients for 2 servings of posset:

1 ⅔ cups (400 ml) fresh whole milk
1 tablespoon honey
1 egg
½ teaspoon cinnamon
½ teaspoon nutmeg
1 pinch mace
Generous ¾ cup (200 ml) dark beer

★

HEAT the milk and honey in a saucepan
until the honey melts.

•

In a large bowl, **BEAT** the egg and spices together.
Slowly incorporate the hot
milk mixture, stirring constantly.

•

Add the freshly opened beer,
and **STIR** vigorously.

•

SERVE IMMEDIATELY.

* 2.2.653–6.

IAGO

Othello is more than a story of jealousy: it's also a drama of manipulation. Despite appearances, the darkest character is really the traitor Iago, who drives Othello to kill his wife Desdemona.

As adviser to Othello, this dishonorable literary figure pulls the strings throughout the play with unabashed wickedness and Machiavellism. Although his motives aren't very clear (a missed promotion), his verbose soliloquies—he monopolizes the stage more than poor Othello—full of bitterness, misogyny, and racism, portray an envious low-ranking officer who destroys lives just for the fun of it. Iago is a "bad guy" with no excuse other than his true depravity.

Othello is more than a theatrical character as far as food is concerned. It's also the name of a grapevine bearing large blue-black fruit. Because of their "foxy" (as though tainted with fox urine) raspberry taste, the organoleptic qualities of these American grapes are somewhat limited. The wine they produced was even prohibited in France from 1935 to 2003 and is now all but forgotten.

IAGO. O, sir, content you; / I follow him to serve my turn upon him: / We cannot all be masters, nor all masters / Cannot be truly follow'd. You shall mark / Many a duteous and knee-crooking knave, / That, doting on his own obsequious bondage, / Wears out his time, much like his master's ass, / For nought but provender, and when he's old, cashier'd: / Whip me such honest knaves. Others there are / Who, trimm'd in forms and visages of duty, / Keep yet their hearts attending on themselves, / And, throwing but shows of service on their lords, / Do well thrive by them and when they have lined / their coats / Do themselves homage: these fellows have some soul; / And such a one do I profess myself. For, sir, / It is as sure as you are Roderigo, / Were I the Moor, I would not be Iago: / In following him, I follow but myself; / Heaven is my judge, not I for love and duty, / But seeming so, for my peculiar end: / For when my outward action doth demonstrate / The native act and figure of my heart / In compliment extern, 'tis not long after / But I will wear my heart upon my sleeve / For daws to peck at: I am not what I am.*

Iago – *Othello*, **Shakespeare** (1604)

* 1.1.41–65.

OTHELLO CAKE

Chocolate lovers have found the color of Othello's skin irresistible. Apparently once a year, for seven years straight, the librettist Arrigo Boito sent Verdi a chocolate cake topped with a miniature of Othello to remind the composer to get to work on the opera that was to prove such a hit in 1887.

Other Othello cakes soon followed: small chocolate-covered cream cakes, like the ones Thomas Mann describes in his memoirs[*]; chocolate sponge cakes filled with vanilla cream (symbolizing the love of Desdemona and the Moor); and chocolate pies topped with candied cherries in Eastern Europe.

In some parts of America, there are even Othello petits fours for each of the main characters: pure chocolate ones for Othello; coffee-filled ones with chocolate icing for Iago; and vanilla cream-filled ones with white chocolate and rose-flavored icing for Desdemona, of course!

Ingredients for 6 servings:

4 ½ oz (125 g) bittersweet baking chocolate
¼ cup (50 ml) whipping cream
3 eggs
½ cup (100 g) sugar
1 teaspoon vanilla extract

5 tablespoons (75 g) lightly salted butter (containing about 5 percent salt), softened
¾ cup (70 g) flour
For the icing:
3 ½ oz (100 g) baking chocolate
1 ½ tablespoons (20 g) butter

Preheat the oven to 390°F (200°C). **BUTTER** an 8-inch (20-cm) round cake pan. Melt the chocolate with the cream over a double boiler.

Separate the egg whites from the yolks, and, off the heat, add the egg yolks to the chocolate mixture.

STIR in the sugar, vanilla extract, softened butter, and flour.

BEAT the egg whites until firm, and pour the chocolate mixture over the beaten egg whites. Fold in gently but thoroughly.

Pour the batter into the pan, and smooth over the top.

BAKE for 20 minutes; then invert the cake onto a platter while still warm. Leave the cake to **COOL** before icing it.

Melt the butter with the chocolate for the icing. Pour the chocolate icing onto the middle of the cake, and **SPREAD** evenly over the top and sides of the cake with a spatula or rounded knife-edge.

CUT INTO EQUAL SLICES!

* 21.

SNOW WHITE'S
STEPMOTHER

Stepmother. One only has to read the word in a fairy tale to feel the fear and dread that it inspires! Instead of merely "a father's second wife," the term has come to mean "a wicked substitute mother." In earlier versions of fairy tales, however, biological mothers often played the part of stepmothers: the stepmother is but the archetypal dark side of the "bad mother."

And the most wicked of stepmothers is without a doubt the queen in *Snow White*. In his analysis, Bruno Bettelheim[*] depicts the story as a search for female identity, a succession of cycles, in which the mother must let her daughter surpass her and take her place.

As long as Snow White is a child, she has nothing to fear. The drama begins when she reaches adolescence: the stepmother refuses to grow old, despite her magic mirror's constant insistence that Snow White has become more beautiful. Snow White's innocence helps her escape from the hunter sent by the queen to fetch her lungs and liver (charming). The poor girl ends up seeking refuge in the home of the hardworking dwarfs. Cleaning, ironing, and other household chores become her daily lot in life—I can already hear the outcry from feminists. The story doesn't say, though, whether or not she also cooks tasty little meals for Grumpy & Co.

On two occasions, the queen tries to assassinate her stepdaughter again, but the dwarfs manage to save her both times. In the end, it's the young girl's ready appetite that does her in.

* Bruno Bettelheim, *The Uses of Enchantment: The Meaning and Importance of Fairy Tales*, 1976.

66

'Snow White shall die,'" she cried, 'even if it costs me my life!'

Thereupon she went into a quite secret, lonely room, where no one ever came, and there she made a very poisonous apple. Outside it looked pretty, white with a red cheek, so that everyone who saw it longed for it; but whoever ate a piece of it must surely die.

When the apple was ready she painted her face, and dressed herself up as a country-woman, and so she went over the seven mountains to the seven dwarfs. She knocked at the door. Snow White put her head out of the window and said, 'I cannot let any one in; the seven dwarfs have forbidden me.' 'It is all the same to me,' answered the woman, 'I shall soon get rid of my apples. There, I will give you one.'

'No,' said Snow White, 'I dare not take anything.' 'Are you afraid of poison?' said the old woman; 'look, I will cut the apple in two pieces; you eat the red cheek, and I will eat the white.' The apple was so cunningly made that only the red cheek was poisoned. Snow White longed for the fine apple, and when she saw that the woman ate part of it she could resist no longer, and stretched out her hand and took the poisonous half. But hardly had she a bit of it in her mouth than she fell down dead. Then the Queen looked at her with a dreadful look, and laughed aloud and said, 'White as snow, red as blood, black as ebony-wood! This time the dwarfs cannot wake you up again.'*

99

The Stepmother – *Snow White*, **The Brothers Grimm, 1812**

* English translation by Margaret Hunt.

BEWITCHING CARAMEL APPLES

Snow White bites into the red half of the apple proffered by her disguised step-mother, who, in turn, bites into the white part. Eating an apple, as Eve so famously did in the Garden of Eden, means putting an end to one's "innocence." (The redness of the forbidden fruit symbolizes the color of blood, menstruation, and eroticism.) Left for dead and buried in a glass coffin, Snow White is finally brought back to life (and sexuality) by the prince, who dislodges the apple that remained literally stuck in her throat. To see the apple as the symbol of the young girl's repressed desires, which she is finally able to accept as she approaches adulthood, only requires a small stretch of the (psychoanalyst's) imagination.

Ingredients for 4 servings:

2 large apples   *A few drops of red food coloring*
Juice of 1 lemon   *Equipment needed:*
1 ⅓ cups (250 g) finely   *melon baller, skewers*
granulated white sugar

PEEL the apples. Using a melon baller, scoop the flesh of
the apples into balls. Sprinkle the fruit with a little
of the lemon juice to prevent it from turning brown.

•

Thread each apple ball onto a **SKEWER**.

•

Fill a large mixing bowl with cold water.

•

Prepare a dry caramel sauce: pour the sugar into a heavy,
dry saucepan, and place over moderate heat.
The sugar will **MELT** and then quickly begin to caramelize.

•

Remove the pan from the heat as soon as the
caramel turns a golden brown color.

•

Because the pan will still be hot, the sauce will continue
to cook. Add the remaining lemon juice, along with the food **COLORING**,
to stop the caramel from cooking further.

•

Dip each apple ball first into the caramel sauce
and then into the **COLD** water to form a hard caramel shell.

•

To serve, insert the apple skewers into an orange or other fruit.

SERVE.

THE OGRE

This star of fairy tales, who appeared under the hand of Charles Perrault in 1697, is in fact a perpetual loser. Hulking and hairy—and well-endowed with a superhuman sense of smell and pointed set of teeth (which end up catching the ogresses off guard)—the Ogre isn't exactly clever and is sometimes outright blind, making it difficult for him to win.

Driven by his senses, the Ogre has a fancy for fresh flesh. But, unlike the wolf, he doesn't bite into it bloody and raw. A sophisticated gourmet, the Ogre likes his flesh tender and well-cooked—rather like the Ogress Queen Mother in Perrault's "The Sleeping Beauty," who asks for her daughter-in-law to be served to her "with a Sauce Robert."* We tend to forget what happens once Princess Aurora gets married—perhaps she would have been better off to have gone on sleeping rather than inherit an ogress for a mother-in-law. Something to remember the next time you complain about yours.

But perhaps an ogre is just a man, after all, who simply eats children rather than the meals you and I enjoy. Thanks to her culinary talent, young Zeralda** manages to steer an ogre away from his cannibalistic tendencies—and even gets him to shave off his beard and marry her!

Be it candied fruits and ladyfingers, Pompano Sarah Bernhardt, or Roast turkey à la Cinderella***: give an ogre haute cuisine, and he will become a man.

* English translation by Robert Samber and J. E. Mansion. A *sauce Robert* is a brown mustard sauce, made with onions, butter, and white wine.
** Tomi Ungerer, *Zeralda's Ogre*, 1967.
*** Menu items that Zeralda serves to her ogre.

"The Ogre first asked if his supper was ready and if the wine was there, and then he sat down at the table. The sheep was still very raw, and it could not have suited him better; but he flourished it about right and left, saying that he smelled fresh flesh. 'It must be that veal that I am about to dress that you smell,' his wife explained.

'I smell fresh flesh! I tell this to you once again,' replied the Ogre, looking at his wife askance; 'and there is something here that I do not understand'; and, saying these words, he got up from the table and went straight to the bed. 'Ah!' said he, 'and this is how you want to deceive me, cursed woman. I don't know what should prevent me from eating you, too; well, perhaps you are too old a beast. Here is some game that has come to me in season to treat my three Ogre friends who are coming to make me a visit.' He drew them, one after another, from underneath the bed.

The poor children fell on their knees before him asking his mercy, but they had to deal with the cruelest of all Ogres, who, far from having any pity for them, was already devouring them with his eyes, and remarked to his wife that they would be delicious morsels with a good sauce of her making.*"

The Ogre — *Hop-o'-My-Thumb*, **Charles Perrault, 1697**

* English translation by Esther Singleton.

42

BEEF PAUPIETTES STUFFED WITH BACON

The original name for this French dish is *Alouettes sans têtes* (literally, "headless larks"), making it the perfect recipe for fooling an ogre. Although the finished product does look a bit like small birds without heads, this typically Provençal recipe calls only for beef, which, thanks to the smoked bacon filling, becomes a scintillating mouthful.

Ingredients for 4 servings:

½-lb (200-g) chunk of smoked bacon, extra-thick
4 cloves garlic, peeled
1 bunch parsley
8 cuts of beef (eye of round or bottom round), thinly sliced
1 large onion, 1 carrot
2 tablespoons olive oil

1 can strained tomatoes (or 2 lb/1 kg fresh tomatoes)
1 sugar cube
Generous ¾ cup (200 ml) white wine
⅔ cup (150 ml) vegetable broth
1 bouquet garni
Salt and pepper
Equipment needed: thin kitchen string

CUT the bacon into 8 pieces. Mince the garlic and parsley.

•

Place a cut of beef onto a cutting board, and on one end, place one of the pieces of bacon and a generous scoop of the garlic-parsley mixture. Add pepper.

•

Roll the beef and filling up to make a paupiette, and TIE tightly with a piece of kitchen STRING. Roll and tie the remaining paupiettes with the rest of the ingredients.

•

Peel and finely CHOP the onion and carrot. Heat the olive oil in a cast-iron casserole, and brown the vegetables and paupiettes on all sides.

•

Add the strained tomatoes, sugar, white wine, broth, and bouquet garni. Season with salt and pepper, and stir.

•

Cover and cook for 1½ hours over low heat, stirring occasionally. If there is too much cooking liquid towards the end, remove the lid, so that it boils down.

•

Serve with tagliatelle.

•

AND REMOVE THE STRING!

THE BIG BAD WOLF

He terrorizes young children, often giving them their first nightmares.

Although he is most famous for his part in Charles Perrault's *Little Red Riding-Hood*, he also plays a leading role in *The Three Little Pigs*, which dates back to the eighteenth century but remains authorless. Originally a folktale, to use the tactful term, this story stars a wolf of varying ferocity, who almost always ends up cooked in a stew. Walt Disney made the fairy tale popular by softening the storyline: in its adaptation, the wolf doesn't manage to gobble down the first two little pigs before breaking his teeth on the cleverest of the three.

Tex Avery used the BBW to symbolize the repressed animal nature, primary instincts, and desires (especially sexual) of man in his comical caricature of the tailcoated ladies' man, completely gaga for a very sexy Little Red Riding Hood. The wolf becomes a man at last!

The Wolf, seeing her come in, said to her, hiding himself under the bedclothes:

'Put the cake, and the little pot of butter upon the bread-bin, and come and lye down with me.'

Little Red Riding Hood undressed herself, and went into bed; where, being greatly amazed to see how her grand-mother looked in her night-cloaths, she said to her:

'Grand-mama, what great arms you have got!'

'That is the better to hug thee, my dear.'

'Grand-mama, what great legs you have got!'

'That is to run the better, my child.'

'Grand-mama, what great ears you have got!'

'That is to hear the better, my child.'

'Grand-mama, what great eyes you have got!'

'It is to see the better, my child.'

'Grand-mama, what great teeth you have got!'

'That is to eat thee up.'

And, saying these words, this wicked Wolf fell upon poor Little Red Riding Hood, and ate her all up.*

The Big Bad Wolf – *Little Red Riding Hood*, **Charles Perrault, 1697** and *The Three Little Pigs*

* **English translation by Robert Samber and J. E. Mansion.**

PIGS IN A BLANKET

These sausage pastries are no doubt too refined for a wolf that prefers eating pigs raw, but what a delicious metaphoric appetizer—for the little piggies!

Ingredients for about 24 tender mouthfuls:

2 ½ cups (240 g) flour
½ teaspoon salt
2 cups (240 g) Greek-style yogurt
½ cup (120 g) butter, softened
2 tablespoons mustard
1 tablespoon honey
1 tablespoon sour cream
6 Strasbourg sausages (or long, thin
butcher's sausages)
1 egg yolk
1 tablespoon milk

Preheat the oven to 350°F (180°C). Line a baking sheet with wax paper.
In a large bowl, mix the flour and salt. Add the yogurt and butter. Combine
thoroughly and knead the resulting dough into a ball.

•

ROLL the dough out onto a floured surface,
so that it is less than a ¼-inch (about 4-to-5-mm) thick.

•

Mix together the mustard, honey, and sour cream in a bowl,
and spread this mixture over the rolled-out dough.

•

Place a sausage on one end of the dough,
and roll the dough twice around the sausage.

•

Cut along the length of the dough, and continue with the
remaining sausages until all six are wrapped with dough.
BEAT the egg yolk with the milk and a pinch of salt, and, with
a pastry brush, spread this mixture over the sausage rolls.

•

With a sharp knife, **CUT** the sausage rolls into bite-size pieces.
Place them on the baking sheet, and cook for 15 to 20 minutes,
or until the little pigs are nice and snug inside their soft eiderdowns.

•

SERVE WARM!

THE COUNT

DE Gernande

It was *Justine* that made the Marquis de Sade's writing known. Justine and Juliette, two orphaned sisters, choose to lead quite different lives: one according to the path of virtue and the other according to vice. Naturally, the virtuous sister is horribly mistreated, while the depraved one gets off easy. After being accused of stealing, raped, branded with a hot iron, and imprisoned by lecherous monks, Justine falls into the hands of the Count de Gernande, who might not exactly be the worst of perverts. This obese gourmand, who inevitably makes one think of an ogre, enjoys bleeding his wife and taking part in orgies.

In *Juliette, or "Vice Amply Rewarded,"* Justine's sister comes across a rather similar character—though even more odious, since Minski, an anthropophagus, likes to be served "'eight or ten virgins-blood sausages and two testicle pastries'"* for breakfast. Justine manages to escape by slipping some stramonium into Minski's hot chocolate.

* Timo Airaksinen, *The Philosophy of the Marquis de Sade*, 147.

The morrow was the Countess' fatal day. Monsieur de Gernande, who only performed the operation after his dinner, which he always took before his wife ate hers, had me join him at table; it was then, Madame, I beheld that ogre fall to in a manner so terrifying that I could hardly believe my eyes....

Two soups were brought on, one a consommé flavored with saffron, the other a ham bisque; then a sirloin of English roast beef, eight hors d'oeuvres, five substantial entrees, five others only apparently lighter, a boar's head in the midst of eight braised dishes which were relieved by two services of entremets, then sixteen plates of fruit; ices, six brands of wine, four varieties of liqueur and coffee. Monsieur de Gernande attacked every dish, and several were polished off to the last scrap; he drank a round dozen bottles of wine, four, to begin with, of Burgundy, four of Champagne with the roasts; Tokay, Mulseau, Hermitage and Madeira were downed with the fruit. He finished with two bottles of West Indies rum and ten cups of coffee.

As fresh after this performance as he might have been had he just waked from sleep, Monsieur de Gernande said:

'Off we go to bleed your mistress; I trust you will let me know if I manage as nicely with her as I did with you.'...

The Countess, dressed only in a loose-floating muslin robe, fell to her knees instantly the Count entered.

"Are you ready?" her husband inquired.

'For everything, Monsieur,' was the humble reply; 'you know full well I am your victim and you have but to command me.'*

The Count de Gernande — *Justine or "Good Conduct Well Chastised,"*
Donatien de Sade (1791)

* 161.

CHOCOLATE MARQUISE CAKE

Sade passed on his relish and passion for food and chocolate to his characters. While locked up in the Bastille, he sent his wife a shopping list for marshmallows, eel pâté, the first strawberries of the season, tuna pâté, and a chocolate cake, "black inside from chocolate as the devil's ass is black from smoke."* The Marquis was very particular about the quality of his chocolate and even went so far as to complain to his devoted wife in 1779: "The sponge cake is not at all what I asked for: 1) I wanted it iced everywhere, both on top and underneath, with the same icing used on the little cookies; 2) I wanted it to be chocolate inside, of which it contains not the slightest hint; they have colored it with some sort of dark herb, but there is not what one could call the slightest suspicion of chocolate. The next time you send me a package, please have it made for me, and try to have some trustworthy person there to see for themselves that some chocolate is put inside. The cookies must smell of chocolate, as if one were biting into a chocolate bar."** Interestingly, at the time, "having one's chocolate" in France meant liking to flirt at parties.

Ingredients for 6 servings:

9 oz (250 g) dark baking chocolate (containing 70 percent cocoa mass)
5 tablespoons (50 g) lightly salted butter (containing about 5 percent salt)
3 tablespoons (50 ml) heavy whipping cream
Whites of 6 organic or free-range eggs, very fresh
2 tablespoons confectioner's sugar

MELT the chocolate over a double boiler.

•

Add the butter away from the HEAT, and stir until the chocolate is smooth and creamy. Add the cream, and stir again.

•

Beat the egg whites until they become mousse-like. Then add the confectioner's sugar, and BEAT again until the egg whites become shiny.

•

Add the chocolate to the egg whites, and fold in gently but thoroughly.

Line a terrine dish (17 fl oz/½ l in volume) with plastic wrap. A cake pan, especially a silicone one, will also do and will make it easier to invert the cake after baking.

•

Pour the batter into the terrine dish, making sure that the top surface is smooth. COVER with plastic wrap, and refrigerate for at least 24 hours.

•

Set the terrine dish in hot water before inverting the cake onto a platter. CUT the cake into thin slices, and serve with whipped cream that has been WHIPPED slowly and conscientiously.

* Sophie D. Coe and Michael D. Coe, *The True History of Chocolate*, 232.
** Marquis de Sade, *Letters From Prison*, 121; English translation by Richard Seaver.

COLOMBA

Colomba della Rebbia isn't a murderess in the strictest sense of the word. She epitomizes the Corsican vendetta. So when her family's sworn enemy, Barricini, assassinates her father and then manages to pull enough crooked strings to be elected mayor and avoid criminal charges, Colomba wants nothing more than to avenge her family in blood.

She eagerly awaits her brother Orso's return, but, as a lieutenant in the Imperial Guard, Orso has changed and cannot imagine himself as a defender of family justice. Since, as a woman, she cannot act alone, Colomba decides to drive her brother to vengeance by using all means possible: adding fuel to the flames and resorting to drama (taking her brother to the scene of the crime and making him believe that his horses have been attacked). A misunderstanding leads Orso up into the mountains with the criminal's two sons. He kills them in a legitimate act of self-defense and, thus, reluctantly fulfills his family's vendetta, to Colomba's immense satisfaction.

Despite being a strong, passionate woman, who fears neither bandits nor bullets nor disobedience, Colomba remains subordinate to the ancestral law of the island and vengeance. With a rare intelligence and strength—unique to all the great vengeful figures of the nineteenth century*—she never questions the justice of her cause.

The symbol of Colomba lives on in Corsica in the form of a white beer flavored with herbs from the island's scrubland. With hints of strawberry, myrtle, and juniper, Colomba was a Bronze Medal Winner at the 2008 Paris Concours Général Agricole.

* For more on this subject: Kris Vassilev, *Le Récit de vengeance au XIXe siècle : Mérimée, Dumas, Balzac, Barbey d'Aurevilly*, 2008.

'Do you know, Colomba,' said Orso, 'Nature blundered when she made you a woman. You'd have made a first-rate soldier.'

'Maybe. Anyhow, I'm going to make my *bruccio*.'

'Don't waste your time. We must send somebody down to warn them and stop them before they start.'

'Do you mean to say you would send a messenger out in such weather, to have him and your letter both swept away by a torrent?... Do you know what you ought to do, Orso? If the storm clears you should start off very early to-morrow morning, and get to our kinswoman's house before they leave it. That will be easy enough, for Miss Lydia always gets up so late. You can tell them everything that has happened here, and if they still persist in coming, why! we shall be very glad to welcome them.'

Orso lost no time in assenting to this plan, and after a few moments' silence, Colomba continued: 'Perhaps, Orso, you think I was joking when I talked of an assault on the Barricini's house. Do you know we are in force—two to one at the very least? Now that the prefect has suspended the mayor, every man in the place is on our side. We might cut them to pieces. It would be quite easy to bring it about. If you liked, I could go over to the fountain and begin to jeer at their women folk. They would come out. Perhaps — they are such cowards! — they would fire at me through their loopholes. They wouldn't hit me. Then the thing would be done. They would have begun the attack, and the beaten party must take its chance. How is anybody to know which person's aim has been true, in a scuffle? Listen to your own sister, Orso! These lawyers who are coming will blacken lots of paper, and talk a great deal of useless stuff. Nothing will come of it all. That old fox will contrive to make them think they see stars in broad midday. Ah! If the prefect hadn't thrown himself in front of Vincentello, we should have had one less to deal with.'

All this was said with the same calm air as that with which she had spoken, an instant previously, of her preparations for making the *bruccio*.[*]

Colomba – *Colomba*,
Prosper Mérimée, 1840

* English translation by Lady Mary Sophia Hely-Hutchinson Loyd.

MINI CORSICAN CHEESECAKES

What do you do with all the leftover whey once you've made your goat's milk or sheep's milk cheese? You make *bruccio*, a traditional cheese made from four parts whey and one part whole goat's or sheep's milk. First, you chill the whey to 41°F (5°C), so that it becomes slightly salty. Then you add the whole milk, and heat the mixture to 167°F (75°C). For the milk to curdle, you need to use something similar to a skimming ladle and carefully transfer the newly formed *bruccio* to a cheese basket to drain. The fresh cheese can then be incorporated into recipes for cannelloni, stuffed vegetables, or traditional *fiadone*. Once it has matured, though, *bruccio* acquires a much stronger taste and becomes *bruccio passu*.

According to legend, it was an ogre that provided the secret recipe for this traditional Corsican cheese. It's the only whey cheese, by the way, to be protected (since 1983) by the French AOC* label. And be careful not to confuse *bruccio* with *brousse* cheese! Real bruccio is never made from cow's milk, whereas *brousse* often is.

Colomba's character was inspired by the real-life story of Colomba Carabelli, a native of Fozzano in southern Corsica, where the traditional bruccio-based pastry is called *imbrucciata* instead of *fiadone*, as it's known in the north.

Ingredients for 6 servings:

1 sheet puff pastry, thawed
3 organic eggs plus 1 egg yolk
½ cup (100 g) sugar
2 cups (500 g) fresh bruccio
Juice and zest of 1 organic, untreated lemon
*2 tablespoons myrtle** or lemon liqueur*
Pinch salt

* *Appellation d'origine contrôlée.*
** You can substitute grappa or even gin.

Roll out the sheet of puff pastry onto a floured cutting
board, so that the dough is about ⅓ inch (1 cm) thick.
CUT six large circles out of the dough. **GREASE** a 6-cup
tartlet pan, and line the cups with the pastry circles.
The circles will overlap the edges of the cups by
¾ inch (2 cm), but don't cut off the surplus dough.
PRICK the bottoms of the pastries with a fork.

•

Preheat the oven to 350°F (180°C).

•

Separate the egg whites from the yolks. **BEAT** three egg
yolks with the sugar, until the mixture turns white.

•

CRUMBLE lthe *bruccio* into the mixture.
Add the zest of the lemon, as well as half its juice and
the liqueur. Stir vigorously.

•

Beat the egg whites with the salt until stiff. Carefully
incorporate them into the above mixture.

•

Distribute the pie filling evenly
among the pastry-lined cups.

•

PINCH the surplus dough between your thumb and
index finger every ¾ inch (2 cm), pulling it toward
the middle, so as to form a scallop design.

•

Bake the mini cheesecakes for 20 minutes.

•

Remove from the oven, and, with a pastry brush,
cover the edges with the remaining egg yolk.

•

Bake for another 10 to 15 minutes,
or until golden-brown. Allow to cool before removing
the cakes from the pan.

REVENGE IS SWEET.

MILADY

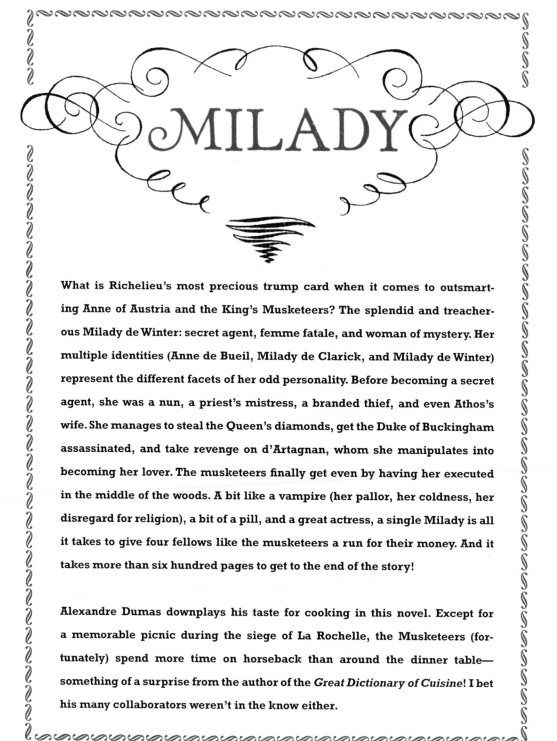

What is Richelieu's most precious trump card when it comes to outsmarting Anne of Austria and the King's Musketeers? The splendid and treacherous Milady de Winter: secret agent, femme fatale, and woman of mystery. Her multiple identities (Anne de Bueil, Milady de Clarick, and Milady de Winter) represent the different facets of her odd personality. Before becoming a secret agent, she was a nun, a priest's mistress, a branded thief, and even Athos's wife. She manages to steal the Queen's diamonds, get the Duke of Buckingham assassinated, and take revenge on d'Artagnan, whom she manipulates into becoming her lover. The musketeers finally get even by having her executed in the middle of the woods. A bit like a vampire (her pallor, her coldness, her disregard for religion), a bit of a pill, and a great actress, a single Milady is all it takes to give four fellows like the musketeers a run for their money. And it takes more than six hundred pages to get to the end of the story!

Alexandre Dumas downplays his taste for cooking in this novel. Except for a memorable picnic during the siege of La Rochelle, the Musketeers (fortunately) spend more time on horseback than around the dinner table—something of a surprise from the author of the *Great Dictionary of Cuisine*! I bet his many collaborators weren't in the know either.

'By the way,' resumed de Winter, stopping at the threshold of the door, 'you must not, Milady, let this check take away your appetite. Taste that fowl and those fish. On my honor, they are not poisoned. I have a very good cook, and he is not to be my heir; I have full and perfect confidence in him. Do as I do. Adieu, dear sister, till your next swoon!'

This was all that Milady could endure. Her hands clutched her armchair; she ground her teeth inwardly; her eyes followed the motion of the door as it closed behind Lord de Winter and Felton, and the moment she was alone a fresh fit of despair seized her. She cast her eyes upon the table, saw the glittering of a knife, rushed toward it and clutched it; but her disappointment was cruel. The blade was round, and of flexible silver.

A burst of laughter resounded from the other side of the ill-closed door, and the door reopened.

'Ha, ha!' cried Lord de Winter; 'ha, ha! Don't you see, my brave Felton; don't you see what I told you? That knife was for you, my lad; she would have killed you. Observe, this is one of her peculiarities, to get rid thus, after one fashion or another, of all the people who bother her. If I had listened to you, the knife would have been pointed and of steel.

Then no more of Felton; she would have cut your throat, and after that everybody else's. See, John, see how well she knows how to handle a knife.'*

Milady – *The Three Musketeers*, **Alexandre Dumas**, 1844

* **Chapter 52.**

CHICKEN CHAUDFROID

Delicate, white, of uncertain origins, typically nineteenth-century, and always cold—the words apply as much to Milady as to this dish. In his *Great Dictionary of Cuisine*, Alexandre Dumas doesn't show much interest in chicken chaudfroid, except as a fricassee with mushrooms and onion, bound with roux and egg yolks, and then put inside a sandwich. Here is a more classic version.

Ingredients for 4 servings:

2 carrots
1 branch celery
½ onion
Handful cloves
4 free-range or organic chicken breasts
1 bay leaf
1 sprig thyme
2 cups (½ l) white wine
1 teaspoon coarse salt
10 peppercorns

For the sauce:
1 teaspoon powdered gelatin (or 2 gelatin leaves)
3 tablespoons (40 g) butter
½ cup (40 g) flour
½ cup (100 ml) crème fraîche or sour cream

For decoration:
fresh herbs and truffle slices

A day ahead:

Peel and slice the carrots, chop the celery, and **STUD** the onion with cloves.

•

Place the chicken breasts, vegetables, salt, peppercorns, and herbs in a cooking pot. Add the white wine and 4 cups (1 l) water. Bring to a boil, and let **SIMMER** for 30 minutes, skimming occasionally.

•

Leave the chicken to cool to room temperature in the broth; then strain and refrigerate for at least 2 hours.

•

Dissolve the powdered gelatin in 4 teaspoons cold water. (If using gelatin leaves, soften them in a bowl of cold water.)

•

STRAIN the broth, and set 2 cups (500 ml) aside.

•

Melt the butter over low heat, and add the flour. Cook for 1 minute, stirring constantly.

Add the 2 cups (500 ml) broth, and let thicken over low heat. Stir constantly for 10 minutes.

•

Add the crème fraîche and gelatin (if using leaves, **WRING** out the excess water first) away from the heat.

•

Season to taste with salt and pepper. Let the béchamel sauce reach room temperature: if it's too warm, it won't set on the chicken breasts; if it's too cold, it will turn lumpy.

•

Apply the chaudfroid sauce to the chicken: place the chilled chicken breasts on a wire rack and use a pastry brush to **COAT** them on all sides with the sauce. Refrigerate for about 1 hour, or until the first coat of sauce sets. Then cover with a second coat of béchamel sauce.

•

Decorate with herbs and slices of truffles before refrigerating again. Remove from the fridge just before serving.

LISA QUENU

She doesn't look mean. The beautiful Lisa Quenu is a pork butcher who looks as tempting in the flesh as her pâtés. But when her brother-in-law, Florent, an escapee from Devil's Island (where he was unjustly sent after the French coup d'état on December 2, 1851), moves in, he disrupts her neat little life whose wheels had been so carefully oiled with lard. With the monstrous Parisian Halles as the backdrop, one thing leads to another, and the battle of the Fat and the Thin is doomed to have casualties. While pretending not to get involved, Lisa denounces Florent and sends her brother-in-law back to Devil's Island in order to maintain her serene way of life. The evidence she gives, however, comes after a pile of anonymous denunciations has already been sent from the entire neighborhood.

" A last memorandum frightened her more than any of the others. It was a half sheet of paper on which Florent had sketched the distinguishing insignia which the chiefs and the lieutenants were to wear. By the side of these were rough drawings of the standards which the different companies were to carry; and notes in pencil even described what colours the banners should assume. The chiefs were to wear red scarves, and the lieutenants red armlets. To Lisa this seemed like an immediate realisation of the rising; she saw all the men with their red badges marching past the pork shop, firing bullets into her mirrors and marble, and carrying off sausages and chitterlings from the window. The infamous projects of her brother-in-law were surely directed against herself—against her own happiness. She closed the drawer and looked round the room, reflecting that it was she herself who had provided this man with a home—that he slept between her sheets and used her furniture. And she was especially exasperated at his keeping his abominable infernal machine in that little deal table which she herself had used at Uncle Gradelle's before her marriage—a perfectly innocent, rickety little table.

For a while she stood thinking what she should do. In the first place, it was useless to say anything to Quenu. For a moment it occurred to her to provoke an explanation with Florent, but she dismissed that idea, fearing lest he would only go and perpetrate his crime elsewhere, and maliciously make a point of compromising them. Then gradually growing somewhat calmer, she came to the conclusion that her best plan would be to keep a careful watch over her brother-in-law. It would be time enough to take further steps at the first sign of danger. She already had quite sufficient evidence to send him back to the galleys.* **"**

Lisa Quenu – *The Fat and the Thin*, **Émile Zola** (**1873**)

* Chapter V, English translation by Ernest Alfred Vizetelly.

MADAME FRANÇOIS'
BACON AND THYME OMELET

Even if food is mentioned on every page of this book, it is hardly in gastronomic terms. *The Fat and the Thin* is more of a fish and cheese encyclopedia than an epicurean feast: be prepared for some stomach-turning indigestion. In order for the thin hero to sit down and eat with pleasure, he needs to leave the stench of Les Halles for the suburb of Nanterre, a true lost paradise, where he can taste a simple dish rich in flavor.

Ingredients for 4 servings:

8 organic or free-range eggs, very fresh
2 tablespoons fresh milk
2 sprigs fresh thyme
½-oz (15-g) piece smoked bacon (a single, thick slice)
Pepper

BREAK the eggs in a large bowl. Add the milk, thyme leaves,
and a few peppermill turns' worth of pepper.
Mix vigorously with a fork, without frothing the eggs.

Remove the layer of fat from the bacon, and put it aside.
CUT the bacon into small chunks, or *lardons*.

Use the bacon fat to **GREASE** a large skillet, and heat.

Pour the egg mixture into the skillet, and let the omelet cook for 3 minutes.

When the surface of the omelet begins to set,
distribute the *lardons* over the runny part of the omelet.

Fold the omelet, so that the *lardons* are in the middle, and heat for another
minute. Serve immediately with a salad and vinaigrette.

The Queen of Hearts

Alice is quite the gourmand! Her adventures begin when she drinks the entire contents of a bottle labeled, "DRINK ME," which makes her shrink: "However, this bottle was NOT marked 'poison,' so Alice ventured to taste it, and finding it very nice, (it had, in fact, a sort of mixed flavour of cherry-tart, custard, pineapple, roast turkey, toffee, and hot buttered toast,) she very soon finished it off."*

Then she eats a cake with the words, "EAT ME," written on top in currants, and she's transformed into a giant.

From the hookah-smoking caterpillar's magic mushroom and the Duchess's cook's pepper soup to turtle soup and the Dormouse in the Mad Hatter's teapot, Alice's appetite is constantly being satisfied or tested.

And with the terrible Queen of Hearts, whose solution to all problems is execution, Alice risks the very worst—but luckily wakes up in time. A steamed rabbit served on a bed of red rose petals would have no doubt overjoyed this despotic sovereign.

* Chapter I.

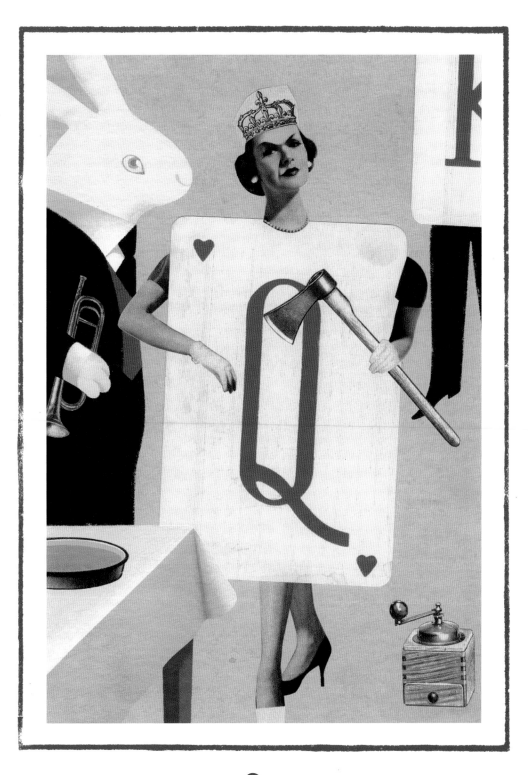

"The King and Queen of Hearts were seated on their throne when they arrived, with a great crowd assembled about them— —all sorts of little birds and beasts, as well as the whole pack of cards: the Knave was standing before them, in chains, with a soldier on each side to guard him; and near the King was the White Rabbit, with a trumpet in one hand, and a scroll of parchment in the other. In the very middle of the court was a table, with a large dish of tarts upon it: they looked so good, that it made Alice quite hungry to look at them—'I wish they'd get the trial done,' she thought, 'and hand round the refreshments! [...]

'Herald, read the accusation!' said the King.

On this the White Rabbit blew three blasts on the trumpet, and then unrolled the parchment scroll, and read as follows:

'The Queen of Hearts, she made some tarts, All on a summer day: The Knave of Hearts, he stole those tarts, And took them quite away!' [...]

The next witness was the Duchess's cook. She carried the pepper-box in her hand, and Alice guessed who it was, even before she got into the court, by the way the people near the door began sneezing all at once.

'Give your evidence,' said the King.

'Shan't,' said the cook.

The King looked anxiously at the White Rabbit, who said in a low voice, 'Your Majesty must cross-examine THIS witness.'

'Well, if I must, I must,' the King said, with a melancholy air, and, after folding his arms and frowning at the cook till his eyes were nearly out of sight, he said in a deep voice, 'What are tarts made of?'

'Pepper, mostly,' said the cook.

'Treacle,' said a sleepy voice behind her."*

The Queen of Hearts *– Alice in Wonderland*, **Lewis Carroll, 1865**

* **Chapter XI.**

TREACLE TART

Treacle is usually an amber-colored syrup also known as golden syrup. Black treacle, which has a licorice taste, is different from ordinary treacle, which has a delicate caramel-honey taste. For the Queen of Hearts' traditional treacle tart, the latter should be used.

The Queen of Hearts shares her love for treacle tart with Harry Potter, who eats some in each of the seven volumes of his saga.

Ingredients for 6 servings:

For the piecrust:	For the filling:
2 cups (200 g) flour	*⅔ cup (240 g) golden syrup*
½ cup (50 g) ground almonds	*¾ cup (100 g) crème fraîche or sour cream*
6 tablespoons (50 g) confectioner's sugar	*½ cup (50 g) dried breadcrumbs*
½ cup (120 g) lightly salted butter	*1 egg*
(containing about 5 percent salt), softened	*Pinch ground ginger*
1 egg, 1 tablespoon milk	*Zest of 1 lemon*

PREHEAT the oven to 350°F (180°C).

•

Prepare the shortbread crust: mix the flour, ground almonds, and confectioner's sugar together. Add the butter, and use your fingertips to incorporate the butter into the flour mixture until the texture becomes sand-like.

•

BEAT the egg and milk together, and add egg mixture to the dough. **KNEAD** with your fingertips until smooth.

•

You can also use a food processor to make the piecrust. Cover the dough with plastic wrap, and refrigerate for 1 hour.

•

Prepare the pie filling in the meantime: mix together the golden syrup, crème fraîche, breadcrumbs, and egg. Add the ginger and lemon zest.

•

To roll out the piecrust, which tends to crumble, use 2 sheets of waxed paper. Roll out the crust to a thickness of about ¼ inch (5 mm), and **PRESS** into a greased pie pan.

•

Pour the filling over the crust, and bake for 40 to 45 minutes.

•

Allow pie to cool before removing from tin.

SERVE CHILLED.

STAVROGIN

How do you describe the complexity of the Russian novel par excellence—rich in both characters and plot—in just a few lines? Some young revolutionaries in a small Russian town want to overthrow the established order. Their despotic leader, Verhovensky, wants the troubled and brilliant aristocrat, Stavrogin, to take the reins of the movement. In the background, a group of supporting characters plods along like chumps. Gradually, Stavrogin, who has everything going for him (looks, strength, intelligence, and nihilism), stirs things up in town: rape, the assassination of a former member of the organization, a fire in a working-class neighborhood while the whole town is at a dance, and the murder of his own wife. In the end, everyone loses, and nothing has any meaning. Unable to forgive himself, Stavrogin commits suicide.

"

A new 'sensation,' another murder! But there was another element in this case: it was clear that a secret society of murderers, incendiaries, and revolutionists did exist, did actually exist. Liza's terrible death, the murder of Stavrogin's wife, Stavrogin himself, the fire, the ball for the benefit of the governesses, the laxity of manners and morals in Yulia Mihailovna's circle.... Even in the disappearance of Stepan Trofimovitch people insisted on scenting a mystery. All sorts of things were whispered about Nikolay Vsyevolodovitch. By the end of the day people knew of Pyotr Stepanovitch's absence too, and, strange to say, less was said of him than of anyone. What was talked of most all that day was 'the senator.' There was a crowd almost all day at Filipov's house. The police certainly were led astray by Kirillov's letter. They believed that Kirillov had murdered Shatov and had himself committed suicide.... It turned out that he knew enough, and presented things in a fairly true light: the tragedy of Shatov and Kirillov, the fire, the death of the Lebyadkins, and the rest of it were relegated to the background. Pyotr Stepanovitch, the secret society, the organisation, and the network were put in the first place. When asked what was the object of so many murders and scandals and dastardly outrages, he answered with feverish haste that 'it was with the idea of systematically undermining the foundations, systematically destroying society and all principles; with the idea of nonplussing every one and making hay of everything, and then, when society was tottering, sick and out of joint, cynical and sceptical though filled with an intense eagerness for self-preservation and for some guiding idea, suddenly to seize it in their hands, raising the standard of revolt and relying on a complete network of quintets, which were actively, meanwhile, gathering recruits and seeking out the weak spots which could be attacked.' In conclusion, he said that here in our town Pyotr Stepanovitch had organised only the first experiment in such systematic disorder, so to speak as a programme for further activity, and for all the quintets—and that this was his own (Lyamshin's) idea, his own theory, 'and that he hoped they would remember it and bear in mind how openly and properly he had given his information, and therefore might be of use hereafter.'[*]

"

Stavrogin – *The Possessed (The Devils)*, **Fyodor Dostoyevsky, 1871**

* English translation by Constance Garnett.

RUSSIAN CUTLETS

You won't find any borscht or pierogi in this novel. No matter what time of day it is—even at breakfast—the main characters are eating cutlets. Beef cutlets? Or lamb? No, not quite: Russian cutlets are like flattened meatballs (made from meat, vegetables, or fish) that are breaded and then pan-fried. Depending on your resources, they can contain varying proportions of breadcrumbs and more noble ingredients.

Ingredients for 4 servings:

2 ½ cups (150 g) fresh breadcrumbs
½ cup (100 ml) milk
1 onion
1 bunch fresh dill
14 oz (400 g) ground meat (beef, chicken, veal, or even salmon) of your choice

1 egg
½ cup (60 g) dried breadcrumbs
3 ½ tablespoons (50 g) butter
Salt and pepper

Soak the fresh breadcrumbs in the milk. Use your hands to **WRING** out any excess liquid.

Then **MINCE** the onion and the dill.

Mix together the ground meat, soaked breadcrumbs, onion, dill, egg, and salt and pepper.

Shape mixture into egg-shaped balls, and **FLATTEN** them between your palms, so that they're about ⅓ inch (1 cm) thick.

Roll these "cutlets" in the dried breadcrumbs, pressing down lightly. **MELT** the butter in a sauté pan, and brown the cutlets on both sides. Lower the heat, and let them **COOK** over low heat. Keep an eye on them (they burn easily because of the breadcrumbs), and drizzle frequently with melted butter.

SERVE PIPING HOT,
with a glass of vodka on the side.

LONG JOHN SILVER

No one would suspect this wooden-legged innkeeper of being a former buccaneer. First he's hired as sea cook (and therefore nicknamed "Barbecue") of a crew that sets off by chance on the trail of buried treasure using Captain Flint's map. Then Long John Silver turns out to be an ex-pirate, determined to retrieve his share of the treasure from his old boss. It's young Jim Hawkins, the novel's hero, who, hidden in an apple barrel, discovers Silver's treacherous plan: to organize a mutiny and claim the treasure for himself. With cunning and manipulation, Long John Silver hides his merciless nature, making him the archetypal pirate who fears neither God nor man and only acts as leader for the lure of money. He's intelligent enough, though, to keep his stash hidden rather than spend it on liquor.

For on Treasure Island, the men drink more than they eat: sometimes brandy but mostly plenty of rum, straight or in a grog: "It's been meat and drink, and man and wife, to me; and if I'm not to have my rum now I'm a poor old hulk on a lee shore."* The staple of their diet is pork and biscuits, hard enough to break your teeth, with some apples thrown in to ward off scurvy. The "plum-duff" that Long John refers to at times is a symbol of la dolce vita on land.

* Chapter 3.

" All the time I was washing out the block house, and then washing up the things from dinner, this disgust and envy kept growing stronger and stronger, till at last, being near a bread-bag, and no one then observing me, I took the first step towards my escapade and filled both pockets of my coat with biscuit.

I was a fool, if you like, and certainly I was going to do a foolish, over-bold act; but I was determined to do it with all the precautions in my power. These biscuits, should anything befall me, would keep me, at least, from starving till far on in the next day....

I went into the cellar; all the barrels were gone, and of the bottles a most surprising number had been drunk out and thrown away. Certainly, since the mutiny began, not a man of them could ever have been sober.

Foraging about, I found a bottle with some brandy left, for Hands; and for myself I routed out some biscuit, some pickled fruits, a great bunch of raisins, and a piece of cheese. With these I came on deck, put down my own stock behind the rudder head and well out of the coxswain's reach, went forward to the water-breaker, and had a good deep drink of water, and then, and not till then, gave Hands the brandy.* "

Long John Silver – *Treasure Island*, **Robert Louis Stevenson, 1883**

SEA BISCUITS

Made from flour, water, lard, and a pinch of salt, sea biscuits are not exactly a treat to make.

For once, instead of using the authentic recipe, I propose a biscuit that tastes of the sea and calls for an ingredient that is, surprisingly, mentioned in the novel: Parmesan cheese.

"'A man who has been three years biting his nails on a desert island, Jim, can't expect to appear as sane as you or me. It doesn't lie in human nature. Was it cheese you said he had a fancy for?'

'Yes, sir, cheese,' I answered.

'Well, Jim,' says he, 'just see the good that comes of being dainty in your food. You've seen my snuff-box, haven't you? And you never saw me take snuff, the reason being that in my snuff-box I carry a piece of Parmesan cheese–a cheese made in Italy, very nutritious. Well, that's for Ben Gunn!'"**

* Chapters 22 and 25
** Chapter 19

SEA BISCUITS

Ingredients for 6 servings:

*3 sheets nori or 3 tablespoons dehydrated
seaweed (found in health food stores)
1 ¾ cups (180 g) flour
½ cup (100 g) freshly grated Parmesan
½ cup (120 g) butter, softened
2 egg yolks, beaten
3 pinches salt flakes*

Preheat the oven to 350°F (180°C).
Line a baking sheet with waxed paper.

•

CUT the nori sheets in small strips with a pair of scissors.

•

Mix together the flour, Parmesan, salt flakes, and seaweed.
Add the butter, and use your fingertips to incorporate the butter
into the flour mixture until the texture becomes sand-like.

•

Make a well in the middle of the dough, and add the egg yolks.
Knead the dough into a ball.

•

Shape the dough into two rolls, and **COVER** in plastic wrap.
Refrigerate for 1 hour.

•

CUT the rolls of dough into ¼-inch (5-mm) thick slices.

•

BAKE for 15 minutes, or until they turn light brown
around the edges.

•

Allow to cool before removing from the baking sheet, and serve
as an appetizer with a glass of rum or whisky.

•

SERVE WHILE SINGING,
"YO-HO-HO, AND A BOTTLE OF RUM!"

EDWARD HYDE

Who exactly is this Mr. Hyde who doesn't blink before beating up children and who likes hanging out in the shadiest of places? Charles Utterson, a lawyer, heads the investigation, which leads him again and again to the home of the good and generous Dr. Jekyll—who has disappeared. The mystery seems unsolvable until Mr. Utterson reads the will that Henry Jekyll has left. The doctor perfected a powerful drug, which transforms him nightly into Edward Hyde (a homophone, of course, of hide). And the dark side, alas, wins out: the doctor can no longer turn back into himself.

A horror novel, this strange adventure was a best seller as soon as it was published and has received many different analyses. Some have read in it the conflict of good and evil in human nature or a psychoanalytical allegory of the conscious and the unconscious—well before the "shadow" of Jungian theory. The double character of Dr. Jekyll and Mr. Hyde has also been thought to emblemize social hypocrisy during the Victorian era, when keeping up moral appearances could hide the worst of vices.

Mr. Hyde's alleged offenses remain pretty blurry (alcohol, shady places, but nothing very concrete). There's not a single woman in the entire book, except for a servant: just lots of men, hidden secrets, blackmail threats, a bachelor's pad, and back doors. Couldn't Jekyll and Hyde's double life be that of a closet homosexual? Or is it just a strange coincidence that the Criminal Law Amendment Act criminalized the "gross indecency" of male homosexuality in the United Kingdom in 1885?

Regardless of the meaning behind this double character, Jekyll/Hyde can be seen as the first superhero: like him, they all have double lives, and dual personalities. The Hulk and Two-Face (the bad guy in Batman) owe him a lot, and even more so the character of Calvin Zabo. A medical researcher obsessed with Stevenson's novel, he keeps trying to reproduce Dr. Jekyll's magic potion. Once transformed into a repulsive creature with superpowers, he calls himself, of course, Mr. Hyde and fights endlessly with Thor and Daredevil.

"Here I proceeded to examine its contents. The powders were neatly enough made up, but not with the nicety of the dispensing chemist; so that it was plain they were of Jekyll's private manufacture; and when I opened one of the wrappers I found what seemed to me a simple crystalline salt of a white colour. The phial, to which I next turned my attention, might have been about half-full of a blood-red liquor, which was highly pungent to the sense of smell and seemed to me to contain phosphorus and some volatile ether. At the other ingredients I could make no guess. The book was an ordinary version-book and contained little but a series of dates. These covered a period of many years, but I observed that the entries ceased nearly a year ago and quite abruptly. Here and there a brief remark was appended to a date, usually no more than a single word: 'double' occurring perhaps six times in a total of several hundred entries; and once very early in the list and followed by several marks of exclamation, 'total failure!!!'....

I hesitated long before I put this theory to the test of practice. I knew well that I risked death; for any drug that so potently controlled and shook the very fortress of identity, might by the least scruple of an overdose or at the least inopportunity in the moment of exhibition, utterly blot out that immaterial tabernacle which I looked to it to change. But the temptation of a discovery so singular and profound, at last overcame the suggestions of alarm. I had long since prepared my tincture; I purchased at once, from a firm of wholesale chemists, a large quantity of a particular salt which I knew, from my experiments, to be the last ingredient required; and late one accursed night, I compounded the elements, watched them boil and smoke together in the glass, and when the ebullition had subsided, with a strong glow of courage, drank off the potion.

Mr. Hyde – *The Strange Case of Dr. Jekyll and Mr. Hyde*, **Robert Louis Stevenson (1886)**

BEET IN A SALT CRUST

For cooks like Dr. Jekyll, it's impossible to practice their art without salt, an extraordinary flavor enhancer. And there within most likely lies the secret to the formula that enables Jekyll to become Hyde:

"My provision of the salt, which had never been renewed since the date of the first experiment, began to run low. I sent out for a fresh supply, and mixed the draught; the ebullition followed, and the first change of colour, not the second; I drank it and it was without efficiency. You will learn from Poole how I have had London ransacked; it was in vain; and I am now persuaded that my first supply was impure, and that it was that unknown impurity which lent efficacy to the draught."

Steaming food in a salt crust allows you to capture flavors that otherwise remain hidden. When you cook beetroots or celery roots in a salt crust, they are revealed in a new light, bringing with them a spectacular dish to the table for you and your guests to discover.

Ingredients for 4 servings:

1 raw beet, about 1 lb (500 g)
4 ½ lb (2 kg) coarse sea salt
2 egg whites
3 teaspoons peppercorns, coarsely ground
1 splash olive oil
1 splash sherry vinegar

Preheat the oven to 350°F (180°C).

•

Wash the beet, and cut off
the top leaves. Don't **PEEL** it.

•

Mix the coarse salt, egg whites,
and ground pepper.

•

Pour a third of the salt mixture
into a round cast-iron casserole.

•

Place the beet in the casserole,
and add the rest of the salt mixture, so that
the beet is completely **COVERED** in salt.

•

Make sure that the sides are well covered.
Cook for 1 hour and 15 minutes.

•

Turn off the oven, and leave the casserole
in the hot oven for another 15 minutes.

•

Take the casserole to the table, and **BREAK**
through the top of the salt crust.

•

Cut the beetroot into 4 pieces, and remove the flesh
with a spoon: it's tender, melts in your mouth, and tastes
incredible–the transformative miracle of salt.

•

Season with olive oil and a bit of sherry vinegar, and

ENJOY

•

*This recipe is also delicious with
a celery root bulb: allow 30 minutes of cooking
time for every 3 ½ oz (100 g) of celery.*

A cynical despot and a trigger-happy, narrow-minded military officer, Ubu has come to symbolize authoritarian delusions and the intoxication of power. Pa Ubu began as a class joke and took off from there. Based on the personality of Mr. Hébert, a physics teacher at Jarry's high school in Rennes, France, the adventures of "Père Heb" were adapted and pushed to the extreme by Jarry, who continued to develop the imaginary character.

An inconsequential dragoon captain, François Ubu (better known by his nick-name, Pa Ubu) lets his wife, Ma Ubu, convince him to kill King Wenceslas and take his place: "If I were you, I'd try to get that bum sitting on a throne. You could become enormously rich, eat as many bangers as you liked, and roll through the streets in a fine carriage."* It's the beginning of Ubu's misfortune: no parallel with Hamlet can be promising.

    The despicable Pa Ubu, characterized by his greed and appetite for money, implements a tax system that resembles a ransom more than a fair and democratic collection. His one incentive? "I'll soon make a fortune: then I'll kill everyone in the world, and go away."** With his "money-tweezers," "lords of phynance, you sons of whores," and "phynancial wheelbarrow" in tow, Pa Ubo goes in person to demand a ransom from the peasants, whose leader is Stanislas Leszczynski. Enter the name of the King of Poland and a breath of sweet air between two resounding "pschitts." Gourmands know that it was indeed one of Stanislas Leszczynski's servants who invented the madeleine and that the Duke of Lorraine himself came up with the wonderful idea of dipping a stale brioche in rum—now known as the rum baba.

A school joke, Ubu Rex is now studied in classrooms and even appears in French dictionaries under "ubuesque," which you can use to say: "Finish your schoup!" to the kids.

---

* English translation by Cyril Connolly and Simon Watson Taylor, 22.
** 43.

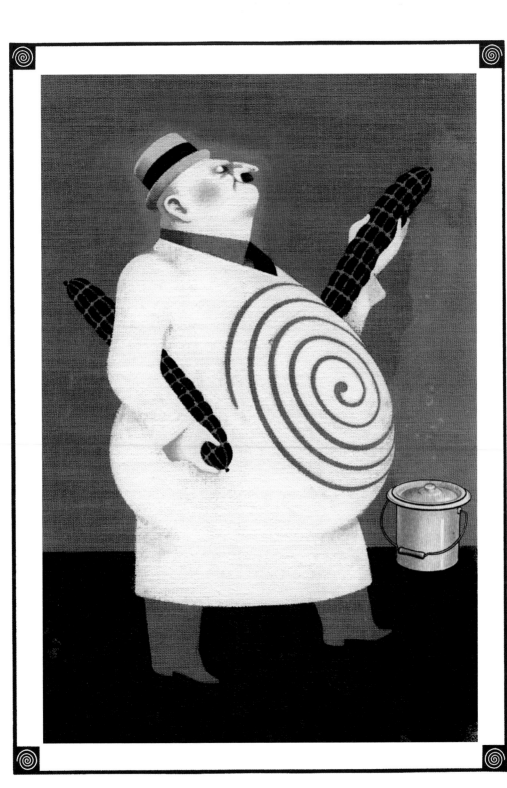

MA UBU. Here's the menu.

PA UBU. That's right up my street.

MA UBU. Polish broth, spare ribs of Polish bison, veal, chicken and hound pie, parsons' noses from the royal Polish turkeys, charlotte russe….

PA UBU. That's enough, I should think. Is there any more?

MA UBU. Ice-pudding, salad, fruit, cheese, boiled beef, Jerusalem fartichokes, cauliflower à la pschitt.

PA UBU. Hey, do you think I'm an oriental potentate, shelling out all that money?

MA UBU. Pay no attention to him. He's off his rocker.

PA UBU. You wait. I shall sharpen my teeth on your shanks.

MA UBU. Just eat up and shut up, Old Ubu! Here, try the Polish broth.

PA UBU. Urghh, what muck!

CAPTAIN MACNURE. You're right. It hasn't quite come off.

MA UBU. Ill-mannered louts, what do you want then?

PA UBU (*clapping his brow*). Ah! I've got an idea. Back in a jiffy. *He goes out.*

MA UBU. Gentlemen, let's try the veal.

CAPTAIN MACNURE. Excellent. What there was of it.

MA UBU. Now for the parsons' noses.

CAPTAIN MACNURE. Absolutely delicious. Hurrah for Ma Ubu!

ALL. Hurrah for Ma Ubu!

PA UBU (*returning*). And soon you'll be yelling hurrah for Old Ubu. *He holds an unmentionable brush in his hand and hurls it at the gathering.*

PA UBU. Try a taste of that. (*Several taste and collapse poisoned.*) Now pass me the spare ribs of Polish bison, Mother, and I'll dish them out.*

Ubu – *Ubu Rex*, **Alfred Jarry, 1896**

* 24.

BUCKWHEAT CRÊPES WITH SAUSAGES

Born in Laval, France, Jarry came up with the character of Ubu with his high school classmates in Rennes. We don't know exactly whether Ubu prefers his sausages from Normandy or Brittany, but when in doubt, it's better to pay tribute to an author's Breton roots. Also, since Ma Ubu's culinary skills seem somewhat limited, it seems safe to choose a simple recipe—and one that calls for a sauté pan, a blunt object that's most effective when it comes to knocking out your enemies... even more so than a "pschitt" brush.

Ingredients for 4 servings (8 crêpes):

1 ½ cups (250 g) buckwheat flour
½ teaspoon salt
3 cups (700 ml) cold water
2 large Roscoff onions (or other sweet onions such as Vidalia)
3 ½ tablespoons (50 g) butter plus 2 tablespoons (30 g) for cooking the crêpes
16 slices of Guéméné* sausage

Make the crêpe batter: mix together the flour and salt,
and make a well in the middle. Add the water,
and stir constantly until the batter is smooth.

•

You can also use a blender to mix the batter.

•

PEEL and **MINCE** the onions. Melt the butter
in a **SAUTÉ** pan, and sauté the onions with a pinch
of salt until they become translucent.

•

Remove the skin from the sausage slices.

•

COOK the crêpes in a greased griddle,
until you have a stack of them.

•

Immediately before serving, melt a pat of butter in the griddle,
and place a crêpe on top. **SPREAD** with some of the sautéed
onions, and top with 2 sausage slices. Fold the crêpe,
and heat for 1 minute. Turn, and heat for another minute.

•

Fold and heat the remaining crêpes with the
rest of the ingredients.

★

AND GOBBLE THEM UP!

* Guéméné is a market town in Brittany known for its andouille, a spicy, smoked pork sausage.

Dracula

Thanks to all the movies and stories inspired by the myth of Dracula, we think we know the vampire's story pretty well. And yet, if you read the work at the source of this myth, you'll be in for a shock. Dracula is a very structured epistolary novel with a wide variety of characters and a subtly disquieting mood that will give you more shivers than most gory horror movies. No fewer than four men are needed to tell the cursed tale to the end.

The Prince of Darkness is far removed from his popular incarnation as a gelled dandy walking along the gutters in a long black satin cape. The count looks like an old man, sporting a long white moustache, aquiline nose, pointy ears, bushy eyebrows, long nails, and hairy palms. He has extraordinary powers, including telepathy and hypnosis, and can command animals and storms, as well as transform himself into a bat or a cloud of mist. No one knows how he became *nosferatu* (literally, "undead"). Could he be the original vampire? After sucking the blood of hundreds of victims, his disappearance seems like a blessing for the world, as well as for himself, as Mina—who manages to escape from his clutches—says: "That poor soul who has wrought all this misery is the saddest case of all. Just think what will be his joy when he, too, is destroyed in his worser part that his better part may have spiritual immortality."

" We left in pretty good time, and came after nightfall to Klausenburgh. Here I stopped for the night at the Hotel Royale. I had for dinner, or rather supper, a chicken done up some way with red pepper, which was very good but thirsty. (Mem. get recipe for Mina.) I asked the waiter, and he said it was called 'paprika hendl,' and that, as it was a national dish, I should be able to get it anywhere along the Carpathians.

I found my smattering of German very useful here, indeed, I don't know how I should be able to get on without it.

I did not sleep well, though my bed was comfortable enough, for I had all sorts of queer dreams. There was a dog howling all night under my window, which may have had something to do with it; or it may have been the paprika, for I had to drink up all the water in my carafe, and was still thirsty. Towards morning I slept and was wakened by the continuous knocking at my door, so I guess I must have been sleeping soundly then.

I had for breakfast more paprika, and a sort of porridge of maize flour which they said was 'mamaliga,' and egg-plant stuffed with forcemeat, a very excellent dish, which they call 'impletata.' (Mem., get recipe for this also.).

The count himself came forward and took off the cover of a dish, and I fell to at once on an excellent roast chicken. This, with some cheese and a salad and a bottle of old tokay, of which I had two glasses, was my supper. "

Dracula – *Dracula*, **Bram Stoker, 1897**

PAPRIKA *HENDL*

Pressed duck? Blood sausage? Such bad taste! Dracula only likes fresh blood! Jonathan Harker, who leaves Exeter to meet with the count at Castle Dracula, discovers Romanian gastronomy en route.

Paprika *hendl*, a Romanian dish, always conjures up Hungarian chicken paprika, which isn't surprising, since Count Dracula's Transylvania belonged to both countries in turn.

Serve this dish with polenta, which is the closest thing to *mamaliga*, paprika hendl's traditional side dish.

Ingredients for 6 servings:

1 large chicken, cut into pieces	2 tablespoons smoked paprika*
2 large onions	1 ¼ cups (150 g) sour cream
2 tablespoons (30 g) butter	2 tablespoons flour
1 can peeled tomatoes	Salt

Season the chicken with salt. **MINCE** the onions.

Melt the butter in a cast-iron casserole, and sauté the onions.

Add the chicken, and brown on all sides.

Add the **PEELED** tomatoes and half the paprika. If necessary, add water, so that the chicken is completed **COVERED** with liquid. Cook for 1 hour over very low heat, until the chicken is tender.

Remove the chicken pieces from the casserole, and keep them warm.

Mix together the sour cream, remaining paprika, and flour. Pour this mixture into the casserole, and cook over low heat for 5 minutes, until the sauce thickens.

Pour the sauce over the chicken, and

SERVE WITH POLENTA.

* Smoked paprika is available in McCormick's Gourmet Collection®, at gourmet markets, and at Hungarian and European specialty stores.

ARSÈNE LUPIN

A gentleman-thief, Arsène Lupin prefers the thrill of disguises and clever tricks to the pleasures of the table. Since he's not a gourmand, we rarely see him eat, and in *Arsène Lupin Versus Herlock Sholmes*, he even turns out to be a vegetarian!

In *813*, under the name of Prince Sernine, Arsène Lupin has the upper hand. We even discover that he was leading an incredible double life as chief of the detective-service for four years. But I've already said too much.

'I must congratulate you, baron; you have a first-rate chef.'

'My chef is a woman-cook, prince. I bribed her with untold gold to leave Levraud, the socialist deputy. I say, try this hot chocolate-ice; and let me call your special attention to the little dry cakes that go with it. They're an invention of genius, those cakes.'

'The shape is charming, in any case,' said Sernine, helping himself. 'If they taste as good as they look…. Here, Sirius, you're sure to like this. Locusta herself could not have done better.'

He took one of the cakes and gave it to the dog. Sirius swallowed it at a gulp, stood motionless for two or three seconds, as though dazed, then turned in a circle and fell to the floor dead.

Sernine started back from his chair, lest one of the footmen should fall upon him unawares. Then he burst out laughing:

'Look here, baron, next time you want to poison one of your friends, try to steady your voice and to keep your hands from shaking…. Otherwise, people suspect you…. But I thought you disliked murder?'

'With the knife, yes,' said Altenheim, quite unperturbed. 'But I have always had a wish to poison someone. I wanted to see what it was like.'

'By Jove, old chap, you choose your subjects well! A Russian prince!'

He walked up to Altenheim and, in a confidential tone, said:

'Do you know what would have happened if you had succeeded, that is to say, if my friends had not seen me return at three o'clock at the latest? Well, at half-past three the prefect of police would have known exactly all that there was to know about the so-called Baron Altenheim; and the said baron would have been copped before the day was out and clapped into jail.'

'Pooh!' said Altenheim. 'Prison one escapes from … whereas one does not come back from the kingdom where I was sending you.'

'True, but you would have to send me there first; and that's not so easy.'

'I only wanted a mouthful of one of those cakes.'

'Are you quite sure?'

'Try.'

[…]

He went back to his chair:

'Let's finish our lunch. But as I like proving the virtues to which I lay claim, and as, on the other hand, I don't want to hurt your cook's feelings, just pass me that plate of cakes.'

He took one of them, broke it in two and held out one half to the baron:

'Eat that!'

The other gave a movement of recoil.

'Funk!' said Sernine.

And, before the wondering eyes of the baron and his satellites, he began to eat the first and then the second half of the cake, quietly, conscientiously, as a man eats a dainty of which he would hate to miss the smallest morsel."

Arsene Lupin – *813*, **Maurice Leblanc (1910)**

* **English translation by Alexander Teixeira de Mattos.**

Plums, peaches, medlars, apricots, cherries, and bitter almonds: beware of the pits! They contain amygdalin, which, when ingested, turns into cyanhydric acid. The taste of bitter almonds is similar to that of the dangerous acid because they both contain cyanide.

Depending on the individual and the quantity ingested, cyanhydric intoxication can result in anything from nausea and loss of consciousness to death by asphyxia. Instant death can also occur.

But it's the dose that makes the poison: it would take about thirty to fifty apricot pits, ingested in a very short time period, to put an end to an adult. If the pits are eaten over a period of several hours, there is nothing to fear because the body gradually eliminates cyanhydric acid.

Ingredients for 12 shortbread cakes:

12 apricots
5 tablespoons (40 g) confectioner's sugar
1 cup (100 g) flour
½ cup (40 g) ground almonds
5 tablespoons (80 g) lightly salted

butter (containing about 5 percent salt), softened
1 drop bitter almond extract
1 egg yolk
Confectioner's sugar

REMOVE the pits from the apricots, and reserve the fruit for another recipe: it's the pits we're after here.

•

With a nutcracker, gently CRACK open the apricot pits. Remove the kernels, being careful not to break them, and put them to one side.

•

Mix together the sugar, flour, and ground almonds in a large bowl. Add the softened butter and bitter almond extract.

•

Use your fingertips to incorporate the butter into the flour mixture until the texture becomes sand-like. Add the egg yolk, mixing into a soft dough, and cover with plastic wrap. Refrigerate for 1 hour.

Preheat the oven to 350°F (180°C). Line a baking sheet with wax paper.

•

Remove the dough from the fridge, and shape into little balls with your hands. Roll the balls in confectioner's sugar, and FLATTEN them between your hands until they're about ⅓ inch (1 cm) thick.

•

Top each cake with an apricot kernel.

•

BAKE for 15 minutes, and allow to cool on a wire rack before serving.

CRUNCH

and savor the taste of danger!

FANTÔMAS

"'Fantômas.'
'What did you say?'
'I said: Fantômas.'
'And what does that mean?'
'Nothing.... Everything!'
'But what is it?'
'Nobody.... And yet, yes, it is somebody!'
'And what does the somebody do?'
'Spreads terror!'"*

We'll never know who Fantômas, the "genius of crime," really is or what drives his dogged hatred for the upper classes. In more than forty novels, first published in installments (hence the choppy style and excessive exclamation points), Fantômas and his gang of hooligans pillage, torture, steal, and kill without any qualms. Hot on their tail are Detective Juve (who ends up discovering that Fantômas is his brother) and the reporter, Jérôme Fandor, who falls in love with Hélène, Fantômas's daughter.

A huge success in Europe before World War I, the fiction of Fantômas was soon picked up by surrealists and movie directors, fascinated by this silhouette clad in black from head to toe, with an expressionless face, who sent shivers down your spine. A symbol of absolute evil, contrasted by the good that Juve and Fandor embody, Fantômas's struggle with the detective and reporter is endless.

"Spreading like a mighty pall
Over Paris, over all,
Who's the ghost with sombre eyes,
Silently observed to rise?
Fantômas – a wild surmise:
Is that you, against the skies?"**

Of course, such a man only lives for crime: it would be out of the question for Fantômas to go so far as eat. In any case, does he really need to feed himself?

* English translation by Cranstoun Metcalfe.
** Robert Desnos, *The Ballad of Fantomas*, 1953; English translation by Timothy Adès.

" They both approached an elegantly set corner table in the main dining room of Scott's Restaurant. They slid into their seats, glanced at the menu, and in a bored voice, the more daring of the two ordered: 'Fix us something good, something nice and rather… chic. We've had enough of menus! It's always the same thing!'

Just then, the maître d' leaned over their table.

'Would you gentlemen care to see the wine list?'

The two friends exchanged a look of regret at this suggestion.

'Vichy water,' they ordered.

The maître d' bowed more deeply.

'By the looks of them, these individuals are no doubt common and vulgar,' thought the dignified man, 'but they show incredible indifference and quite a lot of nerve. They are probably rich storekeepers, or else ordinary people who won at the races.'

The maître d' turned on his heel, proud of the trust that the two men showed in him by leaving the creation of the menu up to him, and called out to the waiters.

'You'll serve the two of them: hors-d'œuvres, American-style lobster, quail on toast, sweetbreads with sorrel, cheese, dessert—'

After a moment, the maître d' added:

'And go ahead and pad the bill. They must be a couple of high rollers, so they won't even notice.'

Fantômas – *The Lost Train*, **Pierre Souvestre and Michel Allain** (1912)

TRUFFLED EGGS WITHOUT TRUFFLES

It's almost a magic trick, like Fantômas, endlessly appearing, disappearing, and changing his appearance: serving eggs that taste like truffle but without any of those small distinctive black flecks (no, no, not pepper!) to be found on your guests' plates.

Because eggshells are porous and truffles are particularly fragrant, you just need to put the two together somewhere, long enough ahead of time, in order for the eggs to become filled with the scent of truffles. And save your truffle for another recipe.

Ingredients for 4 servings:

1 black Périgord truffle, about ¾ oz (20 g)
8 organic or free-range eggs
2 tablespoons whipping cream
1 ½ tablespoons (20 g) lightly salted butter
(containing about 5 percent salt)
Salt and pepper

A day (or even 48 hours) ahead:
carefully brush and dry the truffle.

•

Place the truffle and eggs in a glass
airtight container, and close.

•

The next day: **CRACK** the eggs over a large bowl,
and add the cream. Season to taste with salt and pepper.

•

Stir gently, without frothing the eggs.

•

Melt the butter over a double boiler. **POUR** in the egg mixture,
and cook for 5 to 8 minutes, or to desired doneness,
turning the eggs over constantly with a wooden spoon.

•

Serve immediately on small, warm plates.

•

Abracadabra! The eggs taste like truffle,

BUT THERE'S NOT A TRACE
OF TRUFFLE IN SIGHT.

⤳ TOM RIPLEY ⤳

By a stroke of luck, Tom Ripley, a small-time crook, is sent to Italy by a rich American to convince his son, Dickie Greenleaf, to return to the United States. Dickie is indeed having an easy time of it in southern Italy: painting, spending his father's money, and living la dolce vita.

Jealous, no doubt in love, and envious, Tom Ripley gives in to his impulses and kills Dickie. Thus trapped in a vicious cycle that leads him to pass for Dickie, Tom embarks on a series of lies that leaves him unscathed—and, as one thing leads to another, in possession of a handsome fortune.

The talented Mr. Ripley is an immoral chameleon who, thanks to other people's weaknesses, always manages to land on his feet. A deliciously immoral hero, he'll continue his happy and criminal life throughout the course of five novels, which make up the "Ripliad," as it's known by fans. He even lands the ultimate luxury of having his own biography[*] written: the icing on the cake for someone who doesn't even exist.

[*] Paul Pavlowitch, *Tom*, 2005. The author knows all about identity intrigues, since he posed as Émile Ajar, a pseudonym used by his older cousin, Prix Goncourt winner Romain Gary.

66 Tom celebrated that night by going to a Roman nightclub and ordering a superb dinner which he ate in elegant solitude at a candlelit table for two. He did not at all mind dining and going to the theater alone. It gave him the opportunity to concentrate on being Dickie Greenleaf. He broke his bread as Dickie did, thrust his fork into his mouth with his left hand as Dickie did, gazed off at the other tables and at the dancers in such a profound and benevolent trance that the waiter had to speak to him a couple times to get his attention.

He was suddenly ravenous. He was going to have something luscious and expensive to eat—whatever the Grand Hotel's specialty was, breast of pheasant or petto di pollo, and perhaps cannelloni to begin with, creamy sauce over delicate pasta and a good valpolicella to sip while he dreamed about his future and planned where he went from here.

He had a bright idea while he was changing his clothes: he ought to have an envelope in his possession on which should be written that it was not to be opened for several months to come. Inside it should be a will signed by Dickie, bequeathing him his money and his income. Now that was an idea.* **99**

Tom Ripley – *The Talented Mr. Ripley*, **Patricia Highsmith, 1956**

* 116, 180.

When Ripley finds himself obliged to eat Italian cuisine, he's not exactly thrilled—unlike Patricia Highsmith, who delights in making gourmet annotations and red octopus, which repulse Ripley and happen to be the favorite food of the man whose tastes he's forced to assume.

Ingredients for 4 servings:

2 large organic or free-range chicken breasts
½ purple onion
1 tablespoon olive oil
Juice of 2 large organic, untreated lemons
Zest of ½ large organic, untreated lemon
1 tablespoon honey
A few sprigs of thyme
Salt and pepper

Separate the breast meat from the tenderloins. Set aside the tenderloins for another recipe.

•

Butterfly each breast, so that you have 4 thin cutlets. **POUND** with a mallet to make them as flat as possible.

•

MINCE the onion.

•

Heat the olive oil in a pan, and add chicken. **COOK** over high heat for 3 minutes. Turn, and cook for 3 more minutes. Set chicken aside.

Sauté the onion in the pan juices over medium heat. When the onion becomes translucent, add the lemon juice and zest, honey, and thyme. Stir.

•

COOK the chicken breasts in this sauce for 10 minutes, over very low heat, until the liquid reduces.

•

Away from the heat, season to taste with salt and pepper.

SERVE

with an arugula salad.

ENNEMONDE

Ennemonde, a character who appears in one of Giono's last novels, is not easily forgotten. An obese woman with thirteen children, she raises sheep with her insipid husband and runs the entire household with a firm hand. Ennemonde's heart goes haywire the day she meets the Key-to-Hearts, a professional wrestler who weighing in at twenty stone is a mighty match for her.

For the sake of this handsome Greco-Roman wrestler, she discreetly bumps off her husband, who is later found trampled upon by a mule. The happiness in her crime: she and her lover also find a treasure and see to it that all remaining obstacles to their union are eliminated. Apparently crime does pay since "God wanted her to be happy."

" Ennemonde, for want of anything better, was an excellent cook, she devoted herself to it; everything was used—thrushes, plover, young wild boar, hares. They killed two pigs a year, one in the autumn, the other in spring; and someone with foresight might have predicted certain future events on seeing how much Ennemonde enjoyed grinding by hand the mixture of minced liver and fat in the family pork-butchery....

In 1932–3 people in these parts still lived as they had at the beginning of the century. The Hôtel Tilleuls where Ennemonde used to go had kept its traditios, one still ate at the table d'hôte and there was only one dish, from January 1ˢᵗ to New Year's Eve—*bœuf en daube*. It went on cooking without a break for 365 days and 365 nights in an enormous cauldron that hung in the dining-room hearth. The fire was only let out on the night of December 31ˢᵗ to January 1ˢᵗ, when the cauldron was emptied and cleaned and a start made with next year's *daube*; the fire was relit and hey presto! A daube to which hare and boar were added, as the hunt might allow, sometimes even the fox, but carefully and only for the flavour....

Ennemonde took her second bowl of *bœuf en daube* and drank her litre but never ate all her bread. She specially liked the rich golden-brown gravy of melted lard and fresh oil. She used every time to take the precautions of bringing a soup-spoon with her, hidden in her corsage, and she would produce it at table to drink the gravy-like soup. Her iron-hard gums chewed the overcooked meat very well. It was a real blow-out.* "

Ennemonde – *Ennemonde: A Novel*, **Jean Giono, 1968**

* **English translation by David Le Vay, 12, 55, 57.**

PROVENÇAL BEEF STEW

An author with an appetite, Giono sprinkles all his novels with culinary notes—so much so that his daughter compiled quotes and typically Provençal and Italian recipes from her father's work, as well as anecdotes from his life, in a delicious book[*].

Ingredients for 6 servings:

3 ½ lb (1.5 kg) cuts of beef
(cheek or bottom round)
2 large onions
1 tablespoon olive oil or lard
7 oz (200 g) bacon, diced
5 oz (150 g) pork rind
For the marinade:
3 carrots
3 cloves garlic
1 organic orange

1 large onion
1 bottle full-bodied, young red wine
(Côtes du Rhône, Corbières)
½ cup (100 ml) red wine vinegar
2 bay leaves
2 sprigs thyme
4 juniper berries
10 peppercorns
4 cloves
Coarse salt (preferably from the Camargue)

Two days ahead:
• **CUT** the beef into large cubes. Put meat into a cast-iron casserole.

Make the marinade:
• **PEEL** and slice the carrots. Peel and **MASH** the garlic cloves.
Remove zest from the orange in one continuous strip
(about 2 to 2 ⅓ inches/5 to 6 cm long).
• Peel and quarter the onion.
• Pour the wine and vinegar over the meat. Season to taste
with the salt, and add all the herbs, spices, and orange zest.
Cover the casserole, and allow to marinate overnight in the refrigerator.

The day ahead:
• Empty the contents of the casserole into a large container.
• **MINCE** the onions.
• Without washing out the casserole, place it on the stove,
and heat the oil (or melt the lard). Sauté the onions.
• Strain the beef, and return it to the casserole. Brown it on all sides.
Add the pork rind and bacon, and pour the marinade on top.
• Bring to a boil. Then cover and simmer over very low heat,
stirring from time to time, for 4 to 5 hours, or until the meat is tender.
• Serve with macaroni or fresh tagliatelle.

* Sylvie Giono, *Le Goût du bonheur: la Provence gourmande de Jean Giono*, 1994.

CATHY AMES

In this great American fresco, where good meets evil,

the horrible and perplexing Cathy Ames is a diabolical

figure who steals, kills, and strives to destroy every-

thing around her with refinement. Cathy begins stir-

ring things up around her at a very early age by killing

her parents and leaving her own children with their

father before deciding, by choice, to become a prosti-

tute. There doesn't seem to be any redemption in store

for her—some have compared her to a kind of Eve.

" In the kitchen Kate set the supper on two trays. She measured out the French dressing in a cup and poured it on the string bean salad. On Faye's tray she put her favorite cup and set the soup forward on the stove to heat. Finally she took the eye-dropper from her pocket and squeezed two drops of croton oil* on the string beans and stirred it in. She went to her room and swallowed the contents of a small bottle of Cascara Sagrada** and hurried back to the kitchen. She poured the hot soup into the cups, filled the teapot with boiling water, and carried the trays to Faye's room.

'I didn't think I was hungry,' Faye said. 'But that soup smells good.'

'I made a special salad dressing for you,' said Kate. 'It's an old recipe, rosemary and thyme. See if you like it.'

'Why, it's delicious,' said Faye. 'Is there anything you can't do, darling?'*** "

Cathy Ames – *East of Eden*, John Steinbeck 1952

---

* Croton comes from the same family as the castor-oil plant. Its oil was used as a violent purgative.
** Cascara sagrada is the bark from a North American tree known for its laxative properties.
*** 511–12, 250.

CATHY'S DEAD BEAN SALAD

Proceed with caution when cooking with essential oils: you could, despite yourself, turn into Cathy Ames!

Precautions to follow:
– Always use organic, therapeutic-grade essential oils.
– Never serve food prepared with essential oils to pregnant or breastfeeding women, babies, children under the age of eight, or people with allergies.
– As they are extremely concentrated, essential oils are measured down to the drop. Be sure to follow the correct doses!
– Never use essential oils in their pure state: dilute them first in a fatty (oil, melted butter) or sweet (honey, agave syrup) substance.
– In order to preserve their aroma as much as possible, avoid cooking essential oils.

Ingredients for 6 servings:

*One 17-oz (500-g) jar precooked beans
(Borlotti, kidney, or any other kind to
your liking)
3 well-ripened tomatoes
½ bunch flat-leaf parsley
1 tablespoon balsamic vinegar
4 tablespoons olive oil*

*1 drop sweet thyme essential oil
(Thymus vulgaris)
1 drop sweet basil essential oil
(Ocimum basilicum)
2 drops lemon essential oil
(Citrus limonum)
Salt and pepper*

Strain and rinse the beans under warm water. Let them **DRAIN**.

•

Wash the tomatoes, remove the seeds and **DICE**.
Rinse the parsley, and remove and **CHOP** the leaves.

•

Put two pinches of salt and a few grinds
of pepper in the bottom of a large salad bowl.
Add the vinegar, olive oil, and essential oils
(minding the proper doses), and **MIX** carefully.

•

Add the beans, tomatoes, and parsley.
TOSS, and serve immediately.

★

ENJOY

taking your time!

Mary Maloney

Mary, six months' pregnant, has been waiting for her husband to come home from work. We'll never know what he has told her—because in a state of shock, Mary decides to knock him over the head with a frozen leg of lamb. In order to get rid of the murder weapon, what could be better than cooking it and then serving it with a smile to the police officers who have come to hear her statement?

" When she walked across the room she couldn't feel her feet touching the floor. She couldn't feel anything at all—except a slight nausea and a desire to vomit. Everything was automatic now—down the steps to the cellar, the light switch, the deep freeze, the hand inside the cabinet taking hold of the first object it met. She lifted it out, and looked at it. It was wrapped in paper, so she took off the paper and looked at it again.

A leg of lamb.

All right then, they would have lamb for supper. She carried it upstairs, holding the thin bone-end of it with both her hands, and as she went through the living-room, she saw him standing over by the window with his back to her, and she stopped.

'For God's sake,' he said, hearing her, but not turning round. 'Don't make supper for me. I'm going out.'

At that point, Mary Maloney simply walked up behind him and without any pause she swung the big frozen leg of lamb high in the air and brought it down as hard as she could on the back of his head.

She might just as well have hit him with a steel club.

She stepped back a pace, waiting, and the funny thing was that he remained standing there for at least four or five seconds, gently swaying. Then he crashed to the carpet.

The violence of the crash, the noise, the small table overturning, helped bring her out of he shock. She came out slowly, feeling cold and surprised, and she stood for a while blinking at the body, still holding the ridiculous piece of meat tight with both hands.

All right, she told herself. So I've killed him. "

Mary Maloney – "Lamb to the Slaughter," **Roald Dahl, 1953**

LEG OF LAMB WITH GREEN PEAS

Children all over the world know Roald Dahl for *Charlie and the Chocolate Factory*. You would have to have quite a sweet tooth to dream up Willy Wonka's "hot ice creams for cold days" and "eatable marshmallow pillows." But there is talk of food in almost all of Dahl's works—be it the giant's disgusting snozzcumbers in *The BFG* or the bird pie that Mr. Twit drools over in *The Twits*. Small wonder that his books have, in turn, inspired a perfectly wild cookbook*. A recipe for Stickjaw for Talkative Parents is especially sure to delight young readers.

Ingredients for 1 widow and 5 policemen:

2 shallots
2 cloves garlic
1 bunch fresh mint
3 ½ tablespoons (50 g) butter
1 leg of lamb, about 4 lb (1.8 kg) with the bone
½ cup (100 ml) white wine
7 cups (800 g) green peas, frozen or fresh (shelled)
1 sugar cube
Salt and pepper

Preheat the oven to 410°F (210°C).

PEEL and **MINCE** the shallots.

Peel and **MASH** the garlic.
Rinse, dry, and **CHOP** the mint.

Mix half of the mint with
the garlic and butter. Season to
taste with salt and pepper.
Rub the leg of lamb with this
mixture.

In an ovenproof pan, arrange the
leg of lamb on a bed of shallots.
Pour the white wine on top,
and **COOK** for about 1 hour.

Turn the leg of lamb over halfway
through, and drizzle with pan
juices.

In the meantime, **STEAM** the peas
with the sugar cube.
Away from the heat, add the other
half of the mint to the cooked peas.
Season to taste with salt and
pepper.

Once the lamb is done,
SLICE it, and add a few tablespoons
of pan juices to the peas.

SERVE.

* Roald Dahl, Felicity Dahl, and Josie Fison, *Roald Dahl's Revolting Recipes*, 1994.

ANTON VOWL'S ABDUCTOR

E

He's disappeared! Who? Anton Vowl, searching desperately for a "parabola, not fully confocal in form and fanning out into a horizontal dash."[*] They hurry to find him. But what was he running after? As the investigation progresses, disappearances turn into suspicious deaths, and other discoveries come to light. Though they end up finding the culprit, they don't find the "omission, a blank, a void that nobody but him knows about, thinks about, that, flagrantly, nobody wants to know or think about."[**] A novel written without a single "e"—which a number of critics didn't even notice when they first read it—this giant lipogram is more than a vain literary feat.

It's also a novel about the absence of "them" (or "*eux*," a homophone in French of the letter "e"): the author's father and mother, the former killed when Perec was four years old, and the latter deported in 1943 when the author was six. While he wrote this novel, Georges Perec kept a document issued by the French Ministry of War Veterans in his desk drawer. It was an official certificate, reporting his mother, Cyrla Perec née Szulewicz, as missing and presumably dead. She was last seen alive at the Drancy transit camp outside Paris on February 11, 1943.

[*] English translation by Gilbert Adair, 4.
[**] Ibid., 13.

> **"** It's no frugal cold-cut lunch that Augustus puts in front of his trio of companions but a Lucullan orgy of gastronomic, gustatory, and, so to say, Augustatory glory. Its first dish is a *chaud-froid* of ortolans *à la Souvaroff.* No fish, but an *homard au cumin* for which nothing short of a '28 Mouton-Rothschild is thought apt. To follow, a roast gigot in onion gravy, its flavour subtly brought out by a soupçon of basil; and, to accompany that, in conformity with a tradition at La Maison Clifford (as Azincourt is jocularly known among Augustus's visitors), a tasty if not too spicy curry. And whilst this curry is still making its impact, a paprika salad is brought in, bristling with scallions, cardoons and mushrooms, zucchini and bamboo shoots. To fill that famous *trou normand*, a glass of calvados, naturally of first-class quality; and, in fitting conclusion, a scrumptious *parfait au cassis* with which is drunk a fruity Sigalas-Rabaud of a sort to bring a sigh of swooning bliss from Curnonsky.[*] **"**

Anton Vowl's Abductor – *A Void*, **Charles Georges Perec, 1969**

[*] Ibid., 115.

BLACKCURRANT PARFAIT

There's always a rice salad hanging around the pages of George Perec's novels. In his book, *Thoughts of Sorts*, the writer even offers his readers "81 Easy-Cook Recipes for Beginners"* by using combinatorial mathematics to come up with recipes for sole, sweetbreads, and rabbits (both young and old). Perec goes as far as to try to describe everything he ate and drank during a year in an "Attempt at an Inventory of the Liquid and Solid Foodstuffs Ingurgitated by Me in the Course of the Year Nineteen Hundred and Seventy-Four,"** a list that's more amazing than appetizing!

Ingredients for 6 generous hosts:

4 large egg yolks
⅓ cup (120 g) syrup
1⅔ cups (250 g) fresh blackcurrants
¼ cup (50 ml) blackcurrant liqueur
1⅔ cups (400 ml) whipped cream

Make the syrup: Heat ⅓ cup water
together with ¼ cup/50g sugar until
dissolved, then leave to cool.

•

BEAT the egg yolks and sugar syrup
together until the mixture turns white.

In a blender, **MIX** the blackcurrants
with the liqueur, and add this
mixture to the egg preparation.

•

Add the whipped cream
and combine thoroughly.

•

Pour into a mold and **FREEZE** for 12 hours.

•

Invert the parfait,
and **CUT** a slice for everyone.

* English translation by David Bellos.
** From *Species of Spaces and Other Places*; English translation by John Sturrock.

Hannibal Lecter

Hannibal the Cannibal: what a charming nickname for the serial killer-psychiatrist, Hannibal Lecter! When a criminal nicknamed Buffalo Bill starts scalping and skinning young girls, the FBI has no choice but to send young Clarice Starling to try and extract information from him. Hannibal Lecter is not only a serial killer but also a sophisticated gourmet who even writes for cookery publications. What would you say to a census taker's liver cooked with beans?

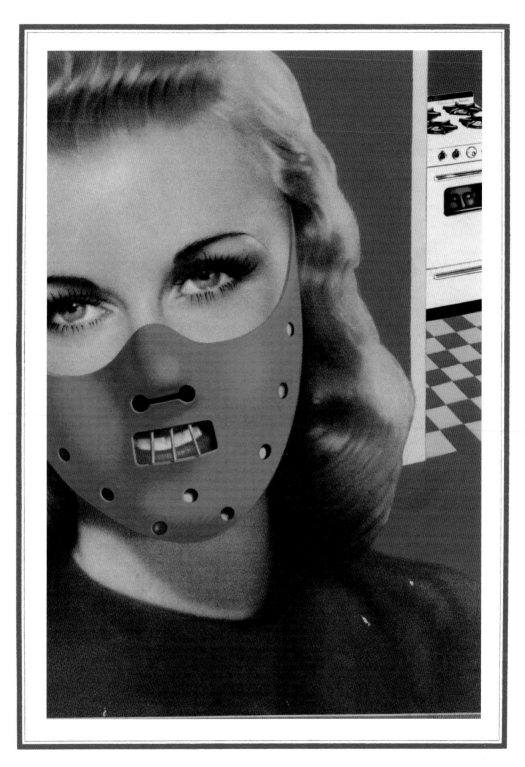

If Hannibal Lecter hadn't decided to study medicine, he might well have been a prized chef or, even worse, a renowned food critic. Where's the proof? He enjoys reading Alexandre Dumas when he's locked up in his prison cell—and not *The Count of Monte Cristo*. For a real escape, he much prefers Dumas' *Great Dictionary of Cuisine*.

Famous for his many articles in gourmet magazines and the quality of his table, Hannibal likes varying the menu but has a marked preference for variety meat. Crunching on one of his victim's cheeks or preparing the thymus of a flutist for a philharmonic orchestra and serving it to his conductor like sweetbreads enthralls him—almost as much as delicately frying the brain of one of Clarice's superiors who had harassed her in butter (from Charentes, France, he likes to point out) right in front of the young FBI agent's astonished, compliant eyes. And Clarice enjoys it: she had never tasted capers before, and they go so well with....

It's not surprising that Hannibal's American creator chose to make him a Frenchman—a synonym for someone with refined taste. For Hannibal is no ogre: he likes eating food raw but prefers it cooked in order to take advantage of cooking's refinements (shopping for cookware at E. Dehillerin, choosing fine china designed by Christofle or Tiffany). The only difference between Hannibal and the rest of us? His "*batterie de cuisine*," which includes an autopsy saw, very useful for cutting bones.

A women's magazine goes so far as to ask him to reveal his best recipes during an interview. It makes you shiver to think what his recipe cards could yield.

Hannibal Lecter – *The Silence of the Lambs*, **Thomas Harris, 1988**

HANNIBAL'S EXPRESS SWEETBREADS

Ingredients for 4 servings:

2 tablespoons (30 g) coarse salt
2 tablespoons white wine vinegar
2 heart* sweetbreads
½ cup (50 g) flour

½ cup (100 g) lightly salted butter
(containing about 5 percent salt)
2 long shallots
¼ cup (50 ml) aged sherry vinegar**
Salt and pepper

Bring 12 cups (3 l) of water to a boil with the coarse salt and white wine vinegar. Blanch the sweetbreads by **PLUNGING** them in the boiling water and allowing them to simmer for 10 minutes. Remove them from the water with a skimming ladle, and allow to cool.

•

With a small knife, remove the sweetbreads' thin skin and membranes—a painstaking task but not especially difficult, especially for anatomy fans.

•

WRAP the sweetbreads in a paper towel, set them on a plate, and press under a weight in order to make firmer. A full carton of milk or juice works well here. The carton's contents aren't important: the weight just needs to be sufficient to flatten the sweetbreads, so that they lose some of their water.

After an hour, wipe the sweetbreads dry, and **SLICE** into thick strips.

•

Pour the flour into a bowl, and add salt and pepper to taste. Gently coat the sweetbread strips with the flour.

•

MELT the butter in a cast-iron skillet, and brown the sweetbreads for 2 minutes. Turn, and brown for another 2 minutes. Place the fried strips on a plate, and cover with another plate to keep warm.

•

PEEL and **MINCE** the shallots.

•

Sauté them in the pan juices until translucent and quite soft (about 5 minutes). Deglaze the pan with the sherry vinegar, and allow shallots to **PICKLE** for a few minutes. Serve the sweetbreads on a bed of the pickled shallots. Season with pepper immediately before serving.

* Sweetbreads consist of two parts: the elongated throat gland (called the *gorge* in French) and the rounder, plumper heart gland (called the *noix* or *pomme* in French).
** "Real" sherry vinegar is protected by the Spanish DO (*denominaciòn de origen*) label. With his attention to detail and elitist tastes, Dr. Lecter would no doubt appreciate the vinegar's delicate nutty flavor.

PatriCk BateMan

For the fun of it, Patrick Bateman, an asocial and thoroughly psychopathic yuppie, uses acid to kill homeless people, prostitutes, and even children in New York at the end of the 1980s. Scenes of dismembering, sophisticated torture, and cannibalism are juxtaposed with smug and ludicrous high-society dinners. Is it all a (nightmarish) dream or an inescapable reality?

" For dinner I order the shad-roe ravioli with apple compote as an appetizer and the meat loaf with chèvre and quail-stock sauce for an entrée. She orders the red snapper with violets and pine nuts and for an appetizer a peanut butter soup with smoked duck and mashed squash which sounds strange but is actually quite good. *New York* magazine called it a 'playful but mysterious little dish' and I repeat this to Patricia, who lights a cigarette while ignoring my lit match, sulkily slumped in her seat, exhaling smoke directly into my face, occasionally shooting furious looks at me which I politely ignore, being the gentleman that I can be. Once our plates arrive I just stare at my dinner—the meat loaf dark red triangles topped by chèvre which has been tinted pink by pomegranate juice, squiggles of thick tan quail stock circling the beef, and mango slices dotting the rim of the wide black plate—for a long time, a little confused, before deciding to eat it, hesitantly picking up my fork.

Even though dinner lasts only ninety minutes it feels as if we have been sitting in Barcadia for a week, and though I have no desire to visit Tunnel afterwards it seems appropriate punishment for Patricia's behavior. The bill comes to $320—less than I expected, actually—and I put it on my platinum AmEx.*"

Patrick Bateman – *American Psycho*, **Bret Easton Ellis, 1991**

* 75–6.

ROAST BEEF WITH TRUFFLED MASHED POTATOES

Ingredients for 6 servings:

1 joint of beef, about 3 lb (1.2 kg)
1 onion
3 ½ lb (1.5 kg) potatoes
1 ¼ cups (300 ml) low-fat milk
½ cup (100 ml) olive oil
1 fresh black truffle, about 1 oz (25–30 g)
Ground nutmeg
Salt and pepper

Remove the beef from the refrigerator about 30 minutes
ahead of time. This will prevent it from shrinking during cooking.
Preheat the oven to 410°F (210°C).

•

Peel and **MINCE** the onion. Spread the minced
onions over the bottom of a lightly greased braising pan.

•

Arrange the roast on this bed, and season lightly with salt and pepper.

•

Cook in the oven for 25 to 40 minutes, depending on
desired doneness (for rare meat, allow 15 minutes of cooking time for the
first pound [500 g] and 10 minutes for every additional pound).

•

PEEL the potatoes, and cook them in a pressure **COOKER**
for 10 minutes, starting from when the valve starts to whistle
(or you can also boil them for 30 minutes).

•

MASH the potatoes with a fork, gradually incorporating
the milk, olive oil, and a pinch of nutmeg.

•

Brush the truffle if this hasn't already been done.

•

Slice the roast, and place the servings of beef and mashed potatoes
onto warm plates. Use a grater to add generous truffle
shavings on top of the mashed potatoes. The heat from the potatoes
will make the aromas breath without weakening them.

•

SERVE IMMEDIATELY.

PRETEXTAT TACH

The obese and repugnant popular writer, Prétextat Tach, knowing that the game is up, invites a few reporters over for some exclusive interviews, which turn into a demolition session. Prétextat sadistically amuses himself with his prey, revolting them with his eating habits that revolve around fat, lard, and alexanders—for which he has perfected a particularly high-calorie recipe. Tach is finally broken and exposed by a young and sharp female reporter who discovers his original crime: strangling his cousin at the start of her teens to prevent her from debasing and ruining herself.

" But in the evening I have a fairly light meal. I'm quite happy with cold dishes, such as rillettes, solidified fat, raw bacon, the oil from a tin of sardines—I don't like the sardines very much, but they flavor the oil, so I throw out the sardines and save the juice, and drink it on its own.... Along with that I cook up a very fatty bouillon, prepared ahead of time: for hours, I boil cheese rind, pig's trotters, chicken rumps, marrowbones, and a carrot. I add a ladleful of lard, remove the carrot, and let it cool for twenty-four hours. In fact, I like to drink the bouillon when it's cold, when the fat has hardened into a crust that leaves my lips glistening.* **"**

Prétextat Tach – *Hygiene and the Assassin*, **Amélie Nothomb, 1992**

* **English translation by Alison Anderson, 2010.**

ALEXANDER WITH CONDENSED MILK

It's the maestro's drink, which he delights in offering every interviewer. His personal touch: replacing the traditional cream with condensed milk and a pat of melted butter. A sure weapon against the cold!

Ingredients for 2 cocktail glasses:

2 ½ tablespoons (40 ml) cognac
2 ½ tablespoons (40 ml) crème de cacao
2 ½ tablespoons (40 ml) condensed milk
Pinch of ground nutmeg
1 pat melted butter

Mix all of the ingredients together
in a cocktail shaker.

SHAKE for 15 seconds.

Pour into cocktail glasses,
and serve immediately.

BOTTOMS UP!

BLAKE/MANZONI

There's no *omertà* on Sicilian cuisine! Its worldwide appreciation has been an unexpected collateral benefit of the mafia's expansion. Giovanni Manzoni (rechristened Blake by the FBI) can't live without his wife Maggie's eggplant Parmesan, which she decides to put on the market—unintentionally causing the entire neighborhood to be ransacked and pillaged.

" To thank the neighbors for doing them a favor, Maggie didn't spare any effort. When the main course was about to be served, her family couldn't resist making a few enticing overtures. Fred said that while he had pretended to marry Maggie for her body, he had really stayed with her for her *melanzane alla parmigiana*. Belle prepared them with a: 'Just wait and see. This thing is sinful,' and Warren, for whom nothing was more boring than neighborly conversations, came to the table just in time for the eggplant. The guests felt compelled to find the dish divine, but they still let themselves be enveloped in a flurry of unknown and contrasting flavors, the fruity, spicy, and well-rounded notes forming a delicate alchemy.

'Maggie, not only is this the best thing I've eaten in my entire life,' said the husband, 'but it's also the best thing I'm ever going to eat.'

'You shouldn't say that in front of your wife, Étienne.'

'I completely agree with him,' his wife interjected. 'My father was a chef at Lepage's in Lyon. I wish he were still alive just to taste your eggplant.'

Maggie knew the passions that her *melanzane alla parmigiana* had unleashed over the years, how many mafiosi would have spat in their mamma's pasta for a serving of her eggplant. Beccegata himself, a restaurant owner for the Manzoni, Polsinelli, and Gallone clans, had removed his parmigiana from the menu after having tasted Maggie's. He had gone down on his knees to ask for her secret, but there simply wasn't any: all of the ingredients, and even the recipe, were known. Only the cook's magic touch could create such a delicious chaos of the palate.* **"**

Blake/Manzoni – *Malavita Encore*, **Tonino Benaquista, 2008**

* **Our translation.**

MAGGIE'S EGGPLANT PARMESAN

Ingredients for a family-size gratin dish:

4 large purple eggplants, about 2 lb (1 kg)
3 tablespoons coarse salt
2 eggs
½ cup (50 g) flour
2 large balls buffalo mozzarella
9 tablespoons (100 g) Parmesan, freshly grated
For the sauce:
1 carrot
1 branch celery
1 sweet onion (yellow or purple)
2 cloves garlic

Olive oil
2 ½ cups (600 ml) tomato sauce
1 teaspoon sugar (or 1 sugar cube)
1 bay leaf
1 sprig thyme
2 tablespoons ordinary balsamic vinegar (not the high-end, ruinously expensive kind that comes in a tiny bottle)
Pinch peperoncino powder (otherwise Espelette pepper will do)
1 tablespoon dried oregano
Salt and pepper

The day ahead: wash, dry, and **SLICE** the eggplants lengthwise into strips, about ⅕ inch (4 mm) thick. **DRAIN** the water from the eggplant strips by sprinkling them with the coarse salt and setting them in a colander. Cover with a plate, and place a weight (such as a canned good or milk carton) on top.

•

The next day: PEEL and chop the carrot, celery, and onion.
Peel and **MASH** the garlic.

•

In a sauté pan, sauté all the vegetables in 1 tablespoon of olive oil. Add the tomato sauce, sugar, bay leaf, and thyme. Let simmer for 20 minutes. Then add the balsamic vinegar, *peperoncino*, and oregano away from the heat.
Preheat the oven to 350°F (180°C).
Firmly **SQUEEZE** remaining water from the eggplant strips,
and wipe them dry with paper towels.

•

Mix together the eggs and flour. **DIP** the eggplant strips in this mixture, and fry them for 2 minutes in very hot olive oil. Turn, and **FRY** for another 2 minutes. Place the fried eggplant strips onto paper towels.

•

Thinly **SLICE** the mozzarella balls.
Grease a large au gratin dish, and line the bottom with a layer of eggplant.
Cover with a layer of mozzarella slices and a layer of tomato sauce.
Continue layering in this order until all ingredients are used.
Top with freshly **GRATED** Parmesan. Bake for 45 minutes.

•

SERVE PIPING HOT.

TEA ROOMS (ALICE IN WONDERLAND)

Le Loir dans la Théière
3 rue des Rosiers - 75004 Paris
Tel: 01 47 72 90 61

•

Alice's Tea Cup
102 West 73rd Street
New York, NY 10023
Tel: (212) 799-3006
www.alicesteacup.com

ROMANIAN GROCERY STORES (DRACULA)

Massis International Foods
4220 43ʳᵈ Avenue, Sunnyside
New York, NY 11104
Tel: (718) 7293749

•

Bacovia Supermarket
296 Neasden Lane, London
NW10 0AD
Tel: 020 7872 320 809

•

Romania Food Centre
198 Station Road, Edgware
London
HA8 7AR
Tel: 020 8958 4442

DELICATESSENS for ITALIAN PRODUCTS (MALAVITA ENCORE)

Italian Food Center
Little Italy
186 Grand Street
New York, NY 10013
Tel: (212) 9252951

•

Lina Stores
18 Brewer Street
Soho, London
W1F 0SH
Tel: 020 7437 6482

RESTAURANTS (EVOLUTION MAN and MACBETH)

St John Bar & Restaurant Smithfield
(for its famous Roast Bone
Marrow & Parsley Salad)
26 St John Street - London
EC1M 4AY
Tel: 020 7251 0848
www.stjohnrestaurant.com

•

Cawdor Castle
Nairn
IV12 5RD
Tel: 01667 404401
info@cawdorcastle.com

CAFÉS (LAMB TO THE SLAUGHTER and SNOW WHITE)

Café Twit at:
The Roald Dahl Museum
& Story Centre
81-83 High Street
Great Missenden
Buckinghamshire
HP16 0AL
United Kingdom
Tel: 01494 892 192
www.roalddahlmuseum.org

•

Snow White Café
6769 Hollywood Blvd
Los Angeles, CA 90028
Tel: (323) 4654444
www.snowwhitecafe.com

RECIPE INDEX

★

★

BIBLIOGRAPHY

Airaksinen, Timo. *The Philosophy of the Marquis de Sade*. London: Taylor & Francis, 1995.

Alighieri, Dante. *The Divine Comedy: Inferno; Purgatorio; Paradiso*. New York: Classic Books International, 2009.

Benacquista, Tonino. *Malavita Encore*.

Bettelheim, Bruno. *The Uses of Enchantment: The Meaning and Importance of Fairy Tales*. London: Thames & Hudson, 1976.

Blanc, Nicole, and Anne Nercessian. *La Cuisine romaine antique*. Grenoble: Glénat, 1992.

Camus, Albert. *The Outsider*. London: Penguin Modern Classics, 2006.

Carroll, Lewis. *Alice's Adventures in Wonderland*. London: Puffin, 2008.

Coe, Sophie D., and Michael D. Coe. *The True History of Chocolate*. London: Thames & Hudson, 1996.

Corneille, Pierre. *The Cid / Cinna / The Theatrical Illusion*. London: Penguin Classics, 1975.

Dahl, Roald. *Charlie and the Chocolate Factory*. London: Puffin, 2007.

——. *The BFG*. London: Puffin, 2007.

——. *The Twits*. London: Puffin, 2007.

——. "Lamb to the Slaughter". From *Skin and Other Stories*. London: Puffin, 2002.

Dahl, Roald, Felicity Dahl, and Josie Fison. *Roald Dahl's Revolting Recipes*. New York: Viking Children's Books, 1994.

Desnos, Robert. *The Ballad of Fantômas*. Translated by Timothy Adès. Papers of Surrealism, 2004.

Dostoyevsky, Fyodor. *The Possessed (The Devils)*. ezReads LLC, 2009.

Dumas, Alexandre. *Dico Dumas : Le Grand dictionnaire d'Alexandre Dumas*. Gallardon: Menu Fretin, 2008.

——. *The Three Musketeers*. London: Puffin Classics, 2003.

Ellis, Bret Easton. *American Psycho*. New York: Vintage, 1991.

Euripides. *Medea*. From *The Plays of Euripides*. BiblioBazaar, LLC, 2010.

Faas, Patrick. *Around the Roman Table: Food and Feasting in Ancient Rome*. New York: Palgrave Macmillan, 2003.

Ferber, Christine, Gilles Laurendon, Laurence Laurendon, Philippe Model, and Bernard Winkelmann. *La Cuisine des fées*. Paris: Editions du Chêne, 2005.

Giono, Jean. *Ennemonde: A Novel*. London: Peter Owen Publishers, 2010.

Giono, Sylvie. *Le Goût du bonheur : la Provence gourmande de Jean Giono*. Paris: Albin Michel, 1994.

Grimm, The Brothers. *Little Snow-White*. From *Household Tales by the Brothers Grimm*. London: George Bell and Sons, 1884.

Harris, Thomas. *The Silence of the Lambs*. New York: St. Martin's Press, 1989.

Highsmith, Patricia. *The Talented Mr. Ripley*. New York: Vintage, 1999.

Homer. *The Odyssey*. Classics Club by William J. Black, Inc., 1994.

Jarry, Alfred. *Ubu Rex*. In *The Ubu Plays: Ubu Rex; Ubo Cuckolded; Ubu Enchained*. New York: Grove Press, 1994.

Kurzke, Hermann. *Thomas Mann: Life as a Work of Art: A Biography*. Princeton: Princeton University Press, 2002.

Lauterbach, Arlette and Alain Raybaud. *Le Livre de cuisine de la Série Noire*. Paris: Gallimard, 1999.

Leblanc, Maurice. *813*. London: Mills & Boon, Limited, n.d, 1913.

Lewis, Roy. *Evolution Man: Or, How I Ate My Father*. New York: Vintage, 1994.

Mérimée Prosper. *Colomba*. Dodo Press, 2008.

Nothomb, Amélie. *Hygiene and the Assassin*. New York: Europa Editions, 2010.

Perec, Georges. *Species of Spaces and Other Places*. London: Penguin Classics, 1998.

——. *Thoughts of Sorts*. Jaffrey: David R. Godine, 2009.

——. *A Void*. New York: HarperCollins Publishers, 1994.

Perrault, Charles. *Hop-o'-My-Thumb*. Translated by Esther Singleton in *The Goldenrod Fairy Book*. Dodo Press, 2010.

——. *Little Red Riding-Hood*. From *Charles Perrault's Classic Fairy Tales*. London: Chancellor, 1986.

——. *The Sleeping Beauty in the Wood*. Ibid.

Piarotas, Mireille, and Pierre Charreton, ed. *Le Populaire à table : Le Boire et le manger aux XIXᵉ et XXᵉ siècles*. Saint-Etienne: Publications de l'Université de Saint-Etienne, 2005.

Pavlowitch, Paul. *Tom*. Paris: Editions Ramsay, 2005.

Sade, Donatien de. *Justine or 'Good Conduct Well Chastised.'* Radford: Wilder Publications, LLC, 2009.

——. *Letters from Prison*. New York: Arcade Publishing, Inc., 1999.

Saint Bris, Gonzague, and Alain Ducasse. *La Grande vie d'Alexandre Dumas*. Paris: Minerva, 2001.

Shakespeare, William. *Titus Andronicus*. London: Penguin Group, 2005.

——. *The Tragedy of Julius Caesar*. London: Penguin Classics, 2005.

——. *The Tragedy of Macbeth*. London: Penguin Classics, 2005.

——. *The Tragedy of Othello, Moor of Venice*. London: Penguin Classics, 2005.

Souvestre, Pierre, and Michel Allain. *Fantômas*. Mineola: Dover Publications, Inc., 2006.

Steinbeck, John. *East of Eden*. London: Penguin Group, 2000.

Stendhal. *The Red and the Black*. London: Penguin Classics, 2002.

Stevenson, Robert Louis. *The Strange Case of Dr. Jekyll and Mr. Hyde*. London: Penguin Classics, 2007.

——. *Treasure Island*. London: Penguin Classics, 2003.

Stoker, Bram. *Dracula*. London: Penguin Classics, 2007.

Suetonius. *The Lives of the Twelve Caesars*. Montana: Kessinger Publishing, 2004.

Tacitus. *Annals*. Macmillan, 1921.

Ungerer, Tomi. *Zeralda's Ogre*. New York: Harper & Row, 1967.

Vassilev, Kris. *Le Récit de vengeance au XIXᵉ siècle : Mérimée, Dumas, Balzac, Barbey d'Aurevilly*. Toulouse: Presses Universitaires du Mirail, 2008.

Zola, Émile. *The Fat and the Thin*. Aegypan, 2007.

ACKNOWLEDGMENTS

Thank you to Philippe for all of his ideas and patience while reading and rereading this book, as well as his sense of humor, and daily support.

Thank you to Fanny Servole-Chavane, Dumé Bergès, Mayalen Zubilaga, Gracianne Nicolas, Caroline Mignot, Patrick Cadour, Adèle Hugot, Caroline Payany, Emmanuel Demercière, Stéphane Girardon, and Laurent Séminel for their ideas and illuminating feedback.

Thank you to Flossie Félix without whom this book would never have been written.

Thank you to Ryma, Aurélie, and Clélia for their patient support throughout this project.

The author would also like to thank the Alexandre Dumas Friends Society, the City of Paris' Detective Literature Library, the Center for Sugar Research and Information (CEDUS), and the Fraîch'Attitude Art Gallery in Paris for granting her access to their documents and archives.

The translator would like to thank her mother, a Francophile and wonderful cook, for all of her helpful input.

Translated from the French by Magda Schmit
Copyediting: Helen Woodhall
Design: 2 Oeufs Bacon P'tites Patates
Typesetting: Barbara Kekus
Proofreading: Chrisoula Petridis
Color Separation: Colorway, Baisieux
Printed in Slovenia by Korotan

Distributed in North America by Rizzoli International Publications, Inc.

Originally published in French as *Les criminels passent à table*
© Flammarion, S.A., Paris, 2010

English-language edition
© Flammarion, S.A., Paris, 2010

editions.flammarion.com

10 11 12   3 2 1

ISBN: 978-2-08-030164-2

Dépôt légal: 09/2010